D145З209

Social Typifications
and the Elusive Other

Social Typifications and the Elusive Other

*The Place of Sociology of Knowledge
in Alfred Schutz's Phenomenology*

Michael D. Barber

WITHDRAWN

Lewisburg
Bucknell University Press
London and Toronto: Associated University Presses

LIBRARY, ST. LAWRENCE UNIVERSITY
CANTON, NEW YORK 13617

HM
22
.G32
S293
1988

© 1988 by Associated University Presses, Inc.

Associated University Presses
440 Forsgate Drive
Cranbury, NJ 08512

Associated University Presses
25 Sicilian Avenue
London WC1A 2QH, England

Associated University Presses
2133 Royal Windsor Drive
Unit 1
Mississauga, Ontario
Canada L5J 1K5

The paper used in this publication meets the requirements
of the American National Standard for Permanence of Paper
for Printed Library Materials Z39.48-1984.

Library of Congress Cataloging-in-Publication Data

Barber, Michael D., 1949–
    Social typifications and the elusive other.

    Bibliography: p.
    Includes index.
    1. Schutz, Alfred, 1899–1959.   2. Phenomenological
sociology.   3. Sociology—Philosophy.   I. Title.
HM22.G32S293   1988   301'.01   86-73241
ISBN 0-8387-5123-7 (alk. paper)

Printed in the United States of America

APR 1 8 1988

To Pat and Dave
and
Maurice Natanson

que me dieron a luz

When you starts measuring somebody, measure him right, child, measure him right. Make sure you done taken account what hills and valleys he come through before he got to wherever he is.

A Raisin in the Sun

Contents

Preface

CONCERNS OF THE sociology of knowledge permeate the philosophical tradition. When the prisoners in Plato's cave resisted the enlightened philosopher descending from above or when the socially sanctioned idols, described by Francis Bacon, blocked access to the truth, sociology of knowledge has manifested its presence in philosophy. The Enlightenment proved itself Bacon's heir by searching for a pure truth, untarnished by irrational, socially induced prejudices, at least until Nietzsche pointed out the irrational roots of the will to pure, rational truth. The philosophical voices of German idealism, particularly Hegel and Marx, played the most prominent role in spawning an independent sociology of knowledge. Just as Hegel found individual appearances only the manifestations of a primordial, pervasive, but often hidden absolute spirit, so Marx understood various knowledge configurations, such as ethics, religion, art, law, or philosophy, as only the manifestations of underlying, concealed production relationships.

Marx in particular has drawn the conceptual map on which the whole succeeding discussion, for the most part, has taken place. According to that map, three elements constitute the sociology of knowledge: the substructure, the superstructure, and the link between them. The substructural factors that determine consciousness include production relations (Marx); drive structures (Ziegler, Salomon); the organization of society (Adler); and *Realfaktoren* (Scheler), such as race, power, and economic relationships. To the superstructure belong the cultural constructs of ethics, religion, art, philosophy, law, and theoretical science. Concerning the link between substructure and superstructure, Robert Merton has suggested that mental productions have been joined to their existential bases by causal relationships (for example, determination, cause, correspondence, necessary condition, conditioning, functional interdependence, interaction, dependence) or by symbolic, organismic, or meaningful relationships (for example, consistency, harmony, coherence, unity, congruence, compatibility, expression, realization, symbolic expression, *Strukturzusammenhang*, structural identities, inner connection, stylistic analogies, logico-meaningful integration, identity of meaning).[1] Talcott Parsons has summarized concisely and criticized the path sociology of knowledge has followed since Marx.

9

It seems to me that the tradition most explicitly associated with the concept of the sociology of knowledge, that in which the names of Marx and Mannheim are most prominent, has operated with too undifferentiated a conceptual scheme. The main framework of the problem has grown out of the tradition of German idealist-historicist thought and has concerned the relations between what are often called *Idealfaktoren* and *Realfaktoren*. The tendency has been to argue over which was the "most important," as for example in the case of Hegel's "idealism" versus Marx's "materialism," and, further, to neglect adequate differentiation of the components on either side of this "equation." Connected with this tendency to dichtomous, either-or thinking has been a strong tendency not to pay adequate attention to the methodological distinction between existential and evaluative judgments, a tendency to relativize all "objectivity" to a base in values or "interests."[2]

As Parsons' final comment indicates, one central problem raised by the sociology of knowledge is whether social conditioning disqualifies any or all claims to truth. Those favoring such forms of sociological relativism, however, seem to lapse into self-contradiction, as the paradox of the sociology of knowledge illustrates. According to that paradox, the thesis that all thinking is socially conditioned and can therefore make no claim to truth, is itself a socially conditioned claim to truth. If all judgments are socially conditioned and therefore false, so also is the judgment that all judgments are socially conditioned and false. Even Mannheim's "relationism," which claims that all thinking is valid relative to a standpoint, seems itself to make the absolute claim that all thinking is valid—relatively.

Alfred Schutz's phenomenology offers a fresh and instructive starting point for reconsidering the tradition, the problems, and the paradox of the sociology of knowledge. First, though, we must keep in mind that Schutz's approach grows out of the three methodological constituents of *The Phenomenology of the Social World:* intentionality, sociality, and essentiality. These three methodological points underpin Schutz's discussion of his predecessors Scheler, Husserl, and Weber (chapter 1). Schutz carefully attends to the intentionality of the Other, rooted, as it is, in the Other's internal time consciousness, his body, and social origins. In Schutz's view, both Husserl and Scheler overlooked the intricacies of the intentionality of the Other. As a result, the difficulties, complexities, and limits of interpersonal understanding elude them. Such an oversight on their part is also consistent with what Schutz believes to be an inadequate integration of the social within their philosophical frameworks. At the same time, Schutz seeks to provide Max Weber's thought with the philosophical foundations and essential definitions that Weber never developed. Schutz's *Phenomenology*, exposited and criticized in chapter 2 of this study, analyzes and describes the intentional structures of consciousness with reference to interpersonal understanding and the structure of the social world. Schutz's unique deployment of phenomenological method discloses the socialized character of the structures of intentionality and makes possible what he calls the "social distribution of knowledge," which takes a step beyond the spatiotemporal distribution of knowledge, the hallmark of the Husserlian account of consciousness (chapter 3). Finally, the Schutzian effort to bring into conjunction intersubjectivity and intentionality in *Phenomenology* unfolds within an eidetic, or essential, account of the life world that can serve as a protosociology (chapter 4) and a protophilosophy (chapter 5).

From this eidetic presentation of the life world in which the intentional structures of consciousness are thoroughly socialized, the following conclusions result: Social-scientific objectivity, defined as reflection on lived experience, finds its limits in the horizonal character of consciousness and in the never to be completely mastered subjective meaning of the Other. In addition, philosophical eidetic claims, the philosophical correlate of social-scientific objectivity, depend on such socially formed lifeworld intentional structures and lie open to two possible investigative responses, distinctive, irreducible to each other, and coherent with Schutz's breakdown of human motivation into "because" and "in-order-to" modes. Through these separate approaches, eidetic claims can be viewed as both socially conditioned and oriented toward truth without contradiction—a conclusion consistent with the Schutzian endeavor to bring into synthesis intentionality and sociality as well as philosophy and sociology.

The preceding conclusions deal with the challenge that the sociology of knowledge raises in regard to sociological and philosophical objectivity. But Schutz's *Phenomenology* also casts the traditional sociology of knowledge, given its initial and continuing direction from Marx, in a new light (chapter 6). The Schutzian view, with its thesis of socialized intentionality, can be employed to dissolve the paradox of the sociology of knowledge, even as it delineates the essential premises that sociological relativism, so often foundering on that paradox, both presupposes and conceals. Finally, Schutz's philosophical position establishes the base of a broader architectonic at whose upper reaches the regular research of the traditional sociology of knowledge can be legitimately and productively carried on. In addition, with Schutz's phenomenology as the eidetic base, the traditional sociology of knowledge can also acquire an epistemological ground, a supplement to its own tendency to abstract from concrete actors, a more intimate relationship to Weberian "interpretive sociology," and a recovery of its own extensiveness and limits.

This study proceeds on a theoretical rather than an empirical plane. It traces the relationship between Schutz's phenomenology and the traditional sociology of knowledge without treating in detail the multiple varieties of past and contemporary sociology of knowledge. It will not examine the entire literature in the field of sociology of knowledge—an enormous part of which is peripheral to the problems considered here— but it will touch on many major figures (for example, Marx, Scheler, and Mannheim) as well as more recent contributors (for example, Merton, Berger and Luckmann, Bloor, and Barnes). Furthermore, this work does not attempt to encompass the broad range of philosophical stances toward the sociology of knowledge or the diverse bridges to the sociology of knowledge from the phenomenological spectrum. However, again, major figures at the intersection of the sociology of knowledge and philosophy/phenomenology, such as Scheler, Merleau-Ponty, Foucault, and Habermas, have received careful attention. Finally, only secondary literature on Schutz deemed relevant to the theme of sociology of knowledge has been explicitly used.

This study profits from a thorough inspection of *The Papers of Alfred Schutz,* a more than eleven-thousand-page archive housed in the Beinecke Rare Book and Manuscript Library at Yale University. This archive consists notably of unpublished manuscripts, lecture and seminar notes for courses Schutz taught at the graduate faculty of the New School for Social Research, and correspondence of philosophical interest, among other things. The archive was most helpful in showing the development of Schutz's thought; Schutz's repeated sensitivity to the distinction between the objective and subjective viewpoints; the extent of attention Schutz paid to Max Scheler; hints that Schutz considered the social sciences to be architectonically arranged with *Phenomenology* as the foundation for higher level, autonomous social sciences; Schutz's awareness of the subtle alteration of experience introduced by reflection on it; the responses that assorted sociological and philosophical topics in Anglo-American thought evoked in Schutz; the applicability of Schutz's thought to literature; Schutz's stress on the *ego agens,* the role of affect in cognition, and the horizonal character of consciousness; and the complexity of Schutz's philosophical relationship to Husserl. A more detailed statement regarding the archive can be found in the Bibliography.

In the course of this book, I will use the masculine personal pronouns *he* and *his* throughout. I follow this policy in the interest of stylistic clarity. I remain in sympathy with the feminist preference for more inclusive language where possible. Similarly, the terms *man* and *fellow man* are used because they were Schutz's own terms and the word *person,* a possible alternative, carries certain ontological connotations (particularly in Scheler's philosophy) that I wished to avoid.

The term *Other* refers to the other human being to whom the *I* relates.

Acknowledgments

I WOULD LIKE to express my thanks to Richard Russell and the Thomas More Center at Yale University for providing an ideal setting for research. I also appreciate the technical support provided by David Wayne. I will always be deeply indebted to Patrick Arnold, the entire family of Felicitas Arteaga, Timothy, Maureen, and Terrance Barber, Gerald Cohen, Mary Commerford, Thomas Kelly, and Ann Ryan. Without the friendship and encouragement of these people, I would never have finished this project.

Thanks are also due Gerhard Böwering, Alma Gonzalez, James McDermott, Kate Keefe, June St. James, Ana Ayala Torres, Lourdes Gomez Torres, and Kathy Vespa for their careful and perceptive proofreading.

I am also indebted to professors Robert Gibbs, Walter Ong, Vincent Punzo, John Smith, and Rulon Wells for their helpful criticisms and frequently expressed interest.

Most of all, I am grateful to Professor Maurice Natanson, who devoted long hours to criticizing this work incisively, repeatedly reviewing it with me, and encouraging me with his humor after devastating me with his critique. My hope is to be half as dedicated to my students' work as he was to mine. Whatever humaneness exists in the following discussion of philosophy of the social sciences is a tribute to Professor Natanson and his own mentor, Alfred Schutz.

I would like to thank the following for permission to make extensive use of their publications:

Doubleday & Company, Inc. for use of Karl Marx, *Writings of the Young Marx on Philosophy and Society,* published by Anchor Books, Doubleday & Company, Inc.

Harper & Row Publishers Inc. for use of Edmund Husserl, *Philosophy as Rigorous Science* in *Phenomenology and the Crisis of Philosophy,* translated with notes and an Introduction by Quentin Lauer, English translation copyright 1965 by Quentin Lauer.

Martinus Nijhoff/Dr. W. Junk publishers for use of Alfred Schutz,

Collected Papers, vols. 1–3 and of Edmund Husserl, *Phenomenological Psy-chology.*

Northwestern University Press for use of Maurice Merleau-Ponty, *Signs* and Alfred Schutz, *The Phenomenology of the Social World,* English language only.

The Modern Schoolman and *Philosophy Today.*

Social Typifications
and the Elusive Other

The Making of the Synthesis:
Schutz's Predecessors

Max Scheler: Collective Persons versus the Other

A REVIEW OF Alfred Schutz's critical assessment of his predecessors Max Scheler, Edmund Husserl, and Max Weber with reference to their handling of the problem of intersubjectivity highlights the components of Schutz's own synthesis—intentionality, sociality, and essentiality. Although Husserl certainly influenced Schutz more than Scheler and chronologically preceded both Schutz and Scheler, Scheler provides a more useful introduction to the discussion of the relationship between Schutz and his predecessors. This is so because Scheler's treatment of the issues of intersubjectivity and the intentionality of the Other proceed relatively unencumbered by the subtleties of phenomenological methodology that accompany Husserl's inquiry into the same topics.

Scheler begins by rejecting the inference by analogy and empathy theories of how we know other minds, a variant of which Wilhelm Dilthey espoused.[1] Scheler's attack on these theories proceeds on many fronts, but two of his central arguments focus on the inconsistency of both theories and on the common fallacies they presuppose. They are inconsistent because they involve a *quaternio terminiorum*. According to this criticism, stated simply, I cannot logically pass from my self to my body, to the existence of bodily gestures of the Other analogous to my own, to the conclusion of another self over there. That other self would be the fourth term. All that I can legitimately conclude is that I myself must exist over there where those bodily gestures analogous to my own are being performed. Further, both the analogy and empathy solutions to the problem of other minds rest on two fallacious assumptions: (1) the first thing given to each of us is his own self and (2) the first thing we can grasp of another human being is the appearance of his body.[2]

Scheler's positive explanation of how intersubjectivity is possible strives to overcome these two fallacies. In regard to the first, Scheler states that there are experiences given to us without any mark indicating the stream of consciousness to which they belong. On the basis of modern child psychology, which reveals that the discovery of the child's own individuality is a relatively late one, Scheler maintains that from the beginning one lives rather in other people's experiences than in his individual sphere. The We is prior to the I. This submersion of the child in a communal whole parallels Scheler's account of the collective person, the *Gesamtperson* (for example, the state, the church, a community) in *Formalism in Ethics and Non-formal Ethics of Values.*[3]

In reference to the second fallacy, Scheler's positive response is to offer his perceptional theory of the alter ego. By that theory, instead of inferring a psychological attitude from a physical gesture we actually perceive in the Other's smile his joy; in his tears, his suffering; in his blushing, his shame; and in his joined hands, his praying.[4]

Although Schutz agrees with Scheler's rejection of the inference by analogy and empathy theories, he opposes his constructive efforts to circumvent the fallacies these theories rest on. Schutz calls Scheler's idea of a hypostasized *Gesamtperson* entirely unclarified, consistently opposes it throughout his writings, and claims that it is in part responsible for Scheler's strange theory that no intentional reflections on acts are possible. Schutz suggests that Scheler's *Gesamtperson* derives from a misuse of eidetic method, his efforts to lend prestige to the Catholic church, and his exaggeration of the principle of solidarity. It is the wrong way to deal with the problem of intersubjectivity.[5]

Furthermore, Schutz criticizes Scheler's perceptional theory of the alter ego. In Schutz's opinion, although I can perceive the superficial attitude exhibited by the other person in his physical expression, I am not given the subjective meaning of the Other. I am not given *why* the other person is exhibiting the attitude he does, his intention in acting. Rather, the bodily movement of the Other is given to me as a state of affairs to be interpreted according to my highly structured context of meaning interpretation of which I am often unaware while it is being applied. The subjective meaning of the Other, which we only approximate in interpretation, is a key concept in Schutz's whole theory of intersubjectivity. Scheler's perceptional theory of the alter ego threatens to ignore it. Similarly, Scheler's first response to the fallacious assumptions of the empathy/analogy theories of other minds, namely, that the We, a communal whole similar to a *Gesamtperson*, is prior to the I, places in jeopardy the uniqueness of the intended meaning of the Other. Little room remains for individual differences among individuals who make up a collective personality.[6]

Concerning this priority of the We to the I, Schutz believes that Scheler is advancing a metaphysical hypothesis (of an all-embracing consciousness prior to the self) in response to a problem that has been

posed by Husserl in the Fifth Cartesian Meditation at the level of transcendental constitution. For Schutz, the problem of intersubjectivity is to
be addressed neither at the level of transcendental constitution nor by
means of metaphysical hypotheses. Rather, it must be treated as a mundane problem, a problem to be disentangled at the level of the natural
attitude, the life world, through a descriptive phenomenological psychology.[7]

At the level of the natural attitude, it is true that the We is prior to the I
in two senses. First, we are born into a world of others who raise us and
bequeath to us typified patterns of knowing and acting. Secondly, I am
often exclusively directed toward the objects of my acts and thoughts,
other persons, but it is possible, at times, to "stop and think"; that is, to
become conscious of my individual self that has been hidden through my
absorption in the objects of my acts and thoughts.[8]

This latency of the self brings to light immediately some of the epistemological difficulties of Scheler's position, for he has failed to distinguish between living in acts and thought directed toward others and
the attitude of reflection on those acts and thoughts. Reflection always
discloses that *my* experiences are *mine*, even though I can be misled into
thinking that these experiences belonged to a We because they were
simply unreflected on. For Schutz, modern studies in the psychology of
children and primitives, such as those by Stern, Ghinn, Lévy-Brühl, and
Koffka, show only that children and primitives live in their acts and
acquire the technique of reflection late—not that they participate in some
primordial *Gesamtperson*.[9]

Schutz's strategies, namely, turning to the natural attitude instead of
reverting to metaphysical hypotheses and distinguishing between living
in acts and reflecting on them, permit Schutz to make his own sense of
Scheler's claim that the We is prior to the I. Schutz goes even further in
trying to account for that priority by appealing to his description of how
we each experience the Other's stream of consciousness in vivid simultaneity in the natural attitude. In the natural attitude, two people, present to each other, witnessing each other's bodily movements, such as
involuntary gestures and facial expressions (which the Other often does
not even perceive about himself), participate in the Other's stream of
consciousness. Insofar, then, as each of us can grasp the Other's
thoughts and acts in the vivid present, whereas either of us can grasp our
own thoughts and acts only as past by way of reflection, it is true to say
that I know more of the Other and he knows more of me than either of
us knows about himself. This present that we share is pregiven to the
self-reflective sphere of the Self; the We is prior to the I.[10]

Also, Schutz's turn to the natural attitude makes possible a reconstruc-
tion of the perceptual theory of the alter ego. For in the natural

attitude, we employ an axiom that Schutz terms the interchangeability of perspectives by which we *assume* that if we interchanged our perspectives we would perceive the same world as the Other. In Schutz's opinion, this axiom of the interchangeability of perspectives, commonly taken for granted in the natural attitude, makes allowance for Scheler's immediate perception of the Other's psychological attitude while not denying the need for more reflective interpretations of the Other whose subjective meaning in its fullness remains a limit.[11]

What is eminently clear, though, is that Schutz's diverse efforts to salvage the Schelerian principle of the priority of the We to the I—his return to the natural attitude, his emphasis on the social transmission of thought-action patterns, his distinction between lived and reflected experience, and his recourse to the we experience in vivid simultaneity—as well as his critical opposition to the perceptional theory of the alter ego enable him to preserve the importance of socialization without sacrificing the uniqueness of the intended meaning of the Other.

Edmund Husserl: Intersubjectivity and the Other

Husserl's most thorough presentation of the constitution of transcendental intersubjectivity and the problems related to it occurs in the Fifth Cartesian Meditation. In the prior meditations, Husserl, employing phenomenological *epoché* in order to withdraw from immersion in the world to bring to light subjectivity, has examined the operating intentionality of conscious life and its constituting syntheses, including the constitution of the ego itself in the fourth meditation. Husserl begins the fifth meditation by attempting to eliminate from the thematic field within the already reduced sphere all constitutive activities that are immediately or mediately related to the subjectivity of Others; that is, all products of the sense determining of other subjectivities. In this way, the I reduces the universe of its conscious life to its *own* transcendental sphere, its concrete being as a monad. The ego's entire transcendental field of experience is thus divided into two strata by this new second reduction: into a sphere of what is properly of the ego and a sphere of what is *not* of the ego. Husserl frequently states that my actual and possible experiences *of* the second sphere, every consciousness *of* it, every manner of appearance *of* it belong to the first sphere, the sphere properly of the ego. Only insofar as the very subjectivity of the Other is in this way bracketed are its products screened off from the sphere that is properly of the ego.[12]

The second step, after this second *epoché*, involves the constitution of the Other's I. Within this doubly reduced sphere, my body stands out in distinction from all others because I can control it in action and attribute sensorial fields to it. The Other also appears as a corporeality but as a corporeality that I apprehend as a body, a body of *another*, by a process of appresentative pairing, a form of passive synthesis, an association grounding a unity of similarity. I then transfer the sense *another's living body* to the other corporeality from my awareness of my own body. Husserl adds that for this appresentation to endure and not prove illusory further appresentations must continue to verify it. In other words, this living body of another must manifest behavior *congruent* with its character as the animated body of an Other.[13]

Husserl proceeds in his third step to show that, once the appresentation of another's animate body as that of the Other is given, so also is given everything belonging to the concretization of this other I; that is, his primordial world, his perspective as a *there* that is *here* to him, and so forth. Further, the interchangeability of our standpoints makes possible the establishment of a common temporal form and common nature. Therefore, according to *Ideen II*, we can enter into communication with each other and constitute "personal unities of a higher order," which are associations of subjects and the cultural world.[14]

Finally, it should be stressed that this transcendental intersubjectivity exists purely in me, the meditating ego. It is constituted from my sources of intentionality but in such a manner that it is the *same* transcendental intersubjectivity in every single human being in his intentional experiences.[15]

Schutz criticizes Husserl in several ways. Husserl seems to overlook the uniqueness of my own body in spite of his earlier emphasis on it. In the first place, Husserl argues that my body stands out as *absolutely unique* in contrast to all other objects perceivable in the world. Then, Husserl contradicts himself by holding that my body, given in inner perception and kinaesthetic experience of its functioning, founds an *analogical apprehension* of an Other's living body. Schutz's argument here bears a likeness to Scheler's repudiation of an inference via analogy to other minds. However, for Schutz, the uniqueness of my own experience of my own body blocks the transfer of the sense of another living body to a body supposedly similar to my own.[16]

Furthermore, Schutz's insistence that the knowledge of the Other, including his experience of his body, remains a limit concept places in doubt the empathic transfer of localizations of my own body to the seen body of the Other. Schutz emphasized the limits in our knowledge of the Other as opposed to Scheler's perceptional theory of the alter ego, also; as we shall see, it is central to Schutz's own theory of intersubjectivity. More specifically, Schutz, following Ortega, asks in his essay "Husserl's Importance for the Social Sciences," "How could transference by empathy, as suggested by Husserl, be possible if I am a male and the Other a female?"[17] It is not surprising that immediately preceding this citation of

Ortega, in a section of the essay criticizing aspects of Husserl's thought on intersubjectivity, Schutz also marshalls Merleau-Ponty (and also indirectly Husserl himself) to his support.

> Merleau-Ponty quotes Husserl's letter to Lucien Lévy-Brühl of 1935 in which he stated that, as an anthropological fact, historical relativism incontestably has its legitimate place as a station on the road leading to the intentional analysis of the structure of the social world. And Merleau-Ponty sums up his own position by stating that, from the phenomenological point of view, the social is not merely an object but, first of all, my situation lived through in a vivid present by means of which also the whole historical past becomes accessible to me . . .[18]

This lived character of the social existence and its incontestable relativism parallel the lived experience of our own body in all its uniqueness, which Husserl seems to pass over in his haste to transfer my experience of my body to the Other's experience of his.

For similar reasons, Schutz points out that the third stage in Husserl's transcendental constitution of the Other, the appresentation of the concretization of the Other, remains dubious, since we have at most only limited interpretive access to the Other's stream of subjective processes. The radical uniqueness of each human consciousness, underestimated by Husserl, raises serious questions about the interchangeability of standpoints (at the level of transcendental constitution and not at the level of a natural attitude assumption), the objectivity that is to result from such an interchangeability, and finally the very possibility of any claim that transcendental intersubjectivity constituted from the sources of my intentionality would be the *same* for every (or even *any* other) single human being.[19]

Underlying and sustaining this whole critique of Husserl's second and third steps in the transcendental derivation of the Other is the same Schutzian appreciation of the uniqueness of the subjective meanings of each individual, which had prompted his resistance to the Schelerian absorption of the individual into a We and the perceptional theory of the alter ego. It is no wonder, then, that Schutz also rejects Husserl's idea of personal unities of a higher order, even as he had opposed Scheler's *Gesamtperson*. For Schutz, Husserl's reference to such entities reflects a lack of familiarity with the concrete problems of the social sciences.[20]

Just as Schutz's defense of the uniqueness of the consciousness of the Other did not inhibit him from grasping the importance of human sociality, of the priority of the We to the I, which Scheler had misconceived, so Schutz emphasizes the ontological priority of the social in his discussion of the problematic second *epoché* in the fifth meditation. According to Schutz, the distinction between "products of the sense determining of other subjectivities" that belong to sphere not properly of the ego and our consciousness *of* those same products belonging to the sphere properly of the ego is untenable because the noematic unities of meaning constituted by my intentional acts involve meanings intended by others, which form the ground of sociality. For instance, no doubt a cultural product of another subjectivity, such as Beethoven's Fifth Symphony, would be consigned to the sphere not properly of the ego, although my *consciousness of* Beethoven's Fifth Symphony would belong to the sphere properly of the ego. But an inspection of the noematic contents of my consciousness of Beethoven's fifth would raise the question how I could have ever become conscious of what a symphony was, who Beethoven was, what his Fifth Symphony is in contrast to his ninth, and so forth, if my own consciousness had not been schooled and informed by *other people* who pass on the cultural tradition of Western music and the noematic contents pertinent to it of which I am aware. How could I even have the vocabulary by which I consciously make the necessary distinction between Beethoven and Brahms, a quartet and a symphony, the fifth and the ninth symphonies if *other people* had not taught me to speak?

In brief, *our very consciousness of products of the subjectivity of Others it itself a social product.* Our consciousness of anything presupposes noematic correlates that bear the mark of the social groups to which we belong. The capacity to separate what is properly of the ego from what is not proves to be impossible ultimately if we are sufficiently aware of how totally immersed human consciousness is in the social world. The utter and inescapable social rootedness of our consciousness of, of the concrete intentional structures through which the world and the Other are given to us, is a fundamental insight of the Schutzian perspective and its particular use of phenomenological method, as we shall later see.[21]

Schutz extends this criticism by objecting that Husserl's verification through further appresentations that the living body of the Other acts in congruence with its character as an animated body in fact presupposes unacknowledged, socially acquired standards of what constitutes congruent and normal behavior if one supposedly possesses an animated body. These hidden presuppositions of an intersubjectively determined context point to a preconstituted stratum that requires further clarification and is equivalent for Schutz to the natural attitude. Thus Husserl would seem to be implicitly making use of intersubjective criteria that should have been set out of play by the second *epoché*.[22]

Max Weber and the Need for a Philosophical Base

Weber fully participated in the discussion of the distinction between the *Geisteswissenschaften* and the *Naturwissenschaften*. Like Rickert and Dilthey, Weber claimed that the object of the social sciences differed

from that of the natural sciences and so demanded a different methodological approach. Weber notes that, unlike cells in a physical organ-
ism, individual human beings in social collectivities "attach a subjective
meaning" to their behavior. This subjective meaning of human actors
calls for the method of interpretive understanding to attain sociological
knowledge.

> In the case of social collectivities, precisely as distinguished from
> organisms, we are in a position to go beyond merely demonstrating
> functional relationships and uniformities. We can accomplish some-
> thing which is never attainable in the natural sciences, namely the
> subjective understanding of the action of the component individuals.
> The natural sciences on the other hand cannot do this, being limited
> to the formulation of causal uniformities in objects and events and the
> explanation of individual facts by applying them. We do not "under-
> stand" the behavior of cells, but can only observe the relevant func-
> tional relationships and generalize on the basis of these observations.
> This additional achievement of explanation by interpretive under-
> standing, as distinguished from external observation, is of course
> attained only at a price—the more hypothetical and fragmentary
> character of its results. Nevertheless, subjective understanding is the
> specific characteristic of sociological knowledge.[23]

Earlier in *Economy and Society*, Weber had described sociology, and
there he immediately proceeded to define social action as subjectively
meaningful behavior. For Weber, the very independence and uniqueness
of sociology in relation to the other sciences depend on the notion of
subjective meaning and the interpretive-understanding methodology
through which that meaning is grasped.

> Sociology (in the sense in which this highly ambiguous word is used
> here) is a science concerning itself with the interpretive understanding
> of social action and thereby with a causal explanation of its course and
> consequences. We shall speak of "action" insofar as the acting individ-
> ual attaches a subjective meaning to his behavior—be it overt or covert,
> omission or acquiescence. Action is "social" insofar as its subjective
> meaning takes account of the behavior of others and is thereby ori-
> ented in its course.[24]

Weber's explanation of subjective meaning begins immediately with a
discussion of meaning. Weber never clearly defines the subjective aspect
of meaning, which presumably contrasts with its opposite, objective
meaning. This lack of definition is symptomatic of a problem Schutz will
focus on. Nevertheless, we can see that Weber implicitly presupposes
that the perspective of the observer is objective in relation to that of the
actor whose perspective is subjective. Weber is aware also that the ob-

server encounters limits in his efforts to understand the subjective meaning of the actor.[25] Schutz correctly notes that Weberian sociological method focuses on the subjective "because its goal is to find out what the actor 'means' in his action, in contrast to the meaning which this action has for the actor's partner or a neutral observer."[26] Subjective meaning is the meaning an action has for the actor, as opposed to those meanings deriving from without, from another.

Weber seems more specific in his definition of meaning, as the following negative definition suggests:

> On the other hand processes or conditions, whether they are animate or inanimate, human or non-human, are in the present sense devoid of meaning in so far as they cannot be related to an intended purpose. That is to say they are devoid of meaning if they cannot be related to action in the role of means or ends but constitute only the stimulus, the favoring or hindering circumstances.[27]

To have meaning, then, an action must be related to a purpose.

In Weber's view, it is the role of science not to prescribe or establish the purposes or values that could be chosen as ends to guide human behavior and render it purposeful and rational. Rather, science can only describe such purposes and values. According to Talcott Parsons, it was the great achievement of Weber's "voluntaristic theory of action" to distinguish these values as *independent* variables from heredity and environment.[28]

According to this Weberian account, in *zweckrational* action an actor recognizes a plurality of legitimate different possible ends, weighs the importance of different possible ends, considers the relationship of an end to its secondary consequences, and contemplates the alternative means to an end before choosing a course of action. This contrasts with another kind of rational, purposeful behavior, named *wertrational,* in which the actor orients his total action to a single specific value that is absolute, and to which all other potential values become significant only as means and conditions to its realization. Here, the actor gives little, if any, regard to the consequences or success of his action. Hence, a fanatical anti-Communist, for instance, might resort to any form of repression of others if only Communists can be kept from power. This anti-Communist does not worry about whether his own repression sets dangerous precedents for the future, about whether such repression will ultimately keep the Communists out or generate a backlash that might bring them to power, or about whether his anticommunism constitutes a *worse* alternative to communism. Thus, Weber observes, from the perspective of *zweckrational* behavior *wertrational* behavior can seem irrational.

Although Weber calls both types of action rational, Schutz accurately perceives that Weber considers *zweckrational* behavior as the archetype of meaningful behavior. Schutz writes:

> In the first place, when Weber talks about meaningful behavior, he is thinking about rational behavior and, what is more, "behavior oriented to a system of discrete individual ends" *(zweckrational)*. This kind of behavior he thinks of as the archetype of action. As a matter of fact, this teleological orientation of action is everywhere in Weber the model for meaningful construction—and with good reason from the standpoint of interpretive sociology.[29]

Parsons, who would agree with Schutz's idea that *zweckrational* behavior is archetypal for Weber, suggests that Weber's two types of nonrational behavior, namely, traditional and affectual behavior, were *residual* types, developed less fully and after Weber's construction of the two preceding rational types of behavior.[30] Both of these forms of behavior, which are usually not undertaken for some purpose, some chosen value, but are merely reactive, stand on the boundaries of what can be called meaningful. We might say that for Weber, meaningful action is action undertaken for a value, but the definition is not all that clear, as Schutz notes.[31]

The fundamental insights of Weberian sociology and Husserlian phenomenology converge. Husserl's phenomenological reduction involves stepping back from immersion in the object given to consciousness in order that the intentionality through which that object is given might come to awareness also; for Husserl, philosophy itself could never have been the same afterward. Likewise, Weber urges sociologists to distance themselves from their objective interpretations of the Other sufficiently so that the subjective meaning of the Other might emerge. For Weber, the Other is not a passive object to be observed like any object of the natural sciences but rather a world-interpreting agent, the study of whom entails the birth of the unprecedented and autonomous science of sociology itself. Schutz systematized this convergence between Husserl and Weber.

Schutz, who recollects that he was under the spell of Weber's methodological writings, basically accepts the tools Weber had forged and envisions his own work as providing Weber with some more adequate philosophical foundations.[32] Schutz credits Weber with the vital discovery of the distinction between the subjective and objective viewpoints, a distinction of the utmost value for the sociology of knowledge, as Schutz observes in a criticism of T. S. Eliot.

> But since Eliot chooses to speak as a sociologist he has to be confronted with a basic issue of the social sciences namely the subjective interpre-

tation by the members of the in-group, or in Max Weber's language the meaning which the actor bestows upon his action versus the objective interpretation by a member of the out-group or the meaning which a fellow man's action has for the observer. It is astonishing, that the student of Karl Mannheim has not carefully investigated this problem so fundamental for all sociology of knowledge.[33]

This discovery of the subjective meaning of the individual actor enables Weber to reduce more complex social relationships and structures to elementary forms of individual behavior. Weber's search for these ultimate foundations enables him to eliminate by reinterpretation the realms of "objective mind" handed down via thinkers like Hegel and Dilthey and also those mysterious *Gesamtpersonen* that Schutz criticized in Husserl and Scheler.[34]

But if Weber's discovery of the subjective meaning was really a search for foundations, he did not seek deep enough. As Schutz points out, Weber was interested in epistemological problems only insofar as they bore directly on specialized research or provided tools for such research. Once these tools were attained, he lost interest in the more fundamental problems. Hence, having perceived the need for the distinction between subjective and objective meaning, Weber failed to recognize the further nuances that this very distinction implied. As a result, Weber concluded a rather homogeneous social world in which he suppressed radical differences in meaning structures.

To be sure, Weber distinguishes between the subjectively intended meaning of an action and its objectively knowable meaning. But he recognizes no further distinctions along this line and pays as little attention to the ways in which an interpreter modifies meaning as he does to the conceptual perspectives in which our fellow human beings are given to us. But, as a matter of fact, there are radical differences in the meaning-structure of my own behavior, the behavior of my consociates, which I immediately experience, and the behavior of those who are merely my *contemporaries* or even my *predecessors*, which is known to me quite indirectly. Far from being homogeneous, the social world is given to us in a complex system of perspectives: my partner and I, for instance, have intimate and rich experience of each other as we talk together, whereas we both appear to a detached observer in an aura of "flatness" and "anonymity." The individual takes these perspectival foreshortenings into account in his acts of meaning-establishment and meaning-interpretation, and they are therefore of direct interest to the social sciences. Here we are not referring to differences between the personal standpoints from which different people look at the world but the fundamental difference between my interpretation of my own subjective experience (self-interpretation) and my interpretation of the subjective experiences of someone else.[35]

Weber's own failure to pursue the ramifications of his discovery of the subjective meaning of the Other resulted in a homogenization of the social world, which resembles that too ready screening out of the difference in the subjective meaning of the Other that Schutz detected in Scheler and Husserl.

Not only has Weber been insufficiently attuned to the implications of his uncovering of the subjective meaning of the Other, but he has also not carefully attended to the fundamental concepts he employs. Schutz notes this first of all with reference to Weber's metaphorical expression in the definition of social action that the actor attaches a subjective meaning to a behavior. In Schutz's opinion, this statement suggests that there is a behavior of which we can be conscious but to which we have not yet attached a meaning. But how could there be such a thing as a behavior of which we are conscious but is without meaning? As soon as we designate an experience as a behavior, we have already noticed it, selected it from other experiences, and given it a meaning. There can be no behavior free of meaning to which we later attach a meaning because the very designation of it as a behavior requires a meaning-bestowing act of attention, according to Schutz's theory of consciousness. Language allows us to separate behavior from its meaning and then predicate the latter of the former. Language thereby tricks us into believing that there can be a behavior that does not depend on some meaning construal. Here, the fundamental phenomenological paradigm, that there is no object without a subjective intentional structure through which it is given, reveals an important epistemological oversight of Weber's. Lacking Schutz's theory of consciousness, Weber is unattuned to that hidden interpreting, that primitive selecting and constituting, which is going on when one fallaciously speaks of behavior without meaning attached to it. On the basis of this epistemological error, Schutz opposes Weber's account of action as only that behavior with a meaning attached to it.

For Schutz, on the other hand, both behavior and action have meaning, in that they are both selected and delineated from the stream of consciousness. The difference between the two is that each possesses a specific *kind* of meaning. Schutz argues that *behavior*, or conduct, as he calls it elsewhere, includes all those experiences of activity that we consciously apprehend but lack reference to any future project to be realized. This conduct would include "all kinds of so-called automatic activities of inner or outer life—habitual, traditional, affectual ones," all called by Leibniz the "class of empirical behavior." *Action*, on the other hand, is behavior based on a preconceived project. Schutz also believes that on the horizon of meaning-endowing acts of attention lie such experiences as physiological reflexes, passive reactions provoked by what Leibniz calls the "surf of indiscernible and confused small perceptions" that are never attended to or given meaning and not remembered and presumably can only be known because others inform us of their presence.[36]

But Weber's failure to recognize hidden interpreting, as in the case where one does admit to his own selective constitution of his *own* experience, also mars Weber's approach to intersubjective understanding of the Other. Weber isolates two types of *Verstehen*, or understanding of the Other: direct observational *(aktuelles)* and explanatory *(erklärendes)*, or motivational, understanding. In *aktuellem Verstehen*, we can understand in an observational way the action of a woodcutter, for instance, or of someone who reaches for the knob to shut the door or of someone who aims a gun at an animal. Motivational understanding, on the other hand, seeks to determine the motivation, to place the observed act in an intelligible and more inclusive context of meaning. Hence, by motivational understanding, we come to know that the woodcutter is working for a wage or chopping wood for his own use or just working off a fit of rage.[37]

Schutz criticizes Weber's account of observational understanding as including more than mere observation. The very designation of an action as woodcutting is already an interpretation of it, for the actor, if asked, might think of his action principally as exercising or pretending to chop wood. The hunter might not be aiming the gun at an animal but watching an animal through the sight of the gun. If either of them were asked what they were doing, they might describe it differently, thus interpret it differently, depending on the very words they use to describe it. Such descriptions could indicate that they might all along have been thinking of what they were doing in a slightly different light than an observer. Here Schutz again shows that what Weber thinks to be objectively a given is in reality an object constituted by a particular interpretation.

In addition, Schutz's critique suggests that Weber's observational understanding is carried on from the observer's viewpoint but without paying sufficient heed to the subjective viewpoint of the actor, to what the action in question may be meaning to him. To take cognizance of that subjective meaning could entail redefining activity once thought obvious to any observer. All social science must be undertaken from the viewpoint of an observer, but it remains from its primitive observational beginnings an effort to determine what an action means to the actor.[38]

Schutz also shows that Weber has ignored the presence of an unacknowledged, interpreting subjectivity by criticizing Weber's use of the word *objective meaning* itself. Indeed, the meanings attached to the Other's behavior by an observer are themselves relative to the viewpoint of that observer and thus are not really objective in the sense of detached from any particular perspective. Schutz himself tells us that the world of subjective meaning is never anonymous, for it essentially depends on and finds its place within the operating intentionality of an ego consciousness, my own or someone else's. Thus, Schutz comments in *Collected Papers*, 2: "The terminology is unfortunate because the term 'objective meaning' is obviously a misnomer, in so far as the so-called 'objective' interpretations are, in turn, relative to the particular attitudes of the interpreters and, therefore, in a certain sense, 'subjective.' "[39]

In Schutz's criticism of Weber's theory of motivational understanding, Schutz also objects that Weber fails to separate what Schutz calls *because motives,* which function more as causal determinisms or motives from the past and *in-order-to motives,* which are the ends or series of future events that I seek to bring about.[40] Schutz asserts that Weber's failure to differentiate these two motivational contexts leads him to make the rather strange claim that social action can "be oriented to the past, present, or expected future behavior of others," as if it might be possible to have as a future project (an in-order-to motive) the bringing about of some change in the past behavior of another, a behavior that is already complete. This confusion makes evident Weber's lack of concern with elucidating the basic notions on which he relies.[41]

In fact, Schutz aims at refining all of Weber's ground concepts: the subjective meaning of the Other, action, behavior, *Verstehen,* objective meaning, motivation, and time. Schutz attempts to clarify general meanings of these terms, their eidetic significance, without examining their empirical instantiations. He writes:

> But, imposing as Weber's concept of "interpretive sociology" is, it is based on a series of tacit presuppositions. It is a matter of urgent necessity to identify these presuppositions and to state them clearly, for only a radical analysis of the genuine and basic elements of social action can provide a reliable foundation for the future progress of the social sciences.[42]

In his discussion of Weber, Schutz displays his primary concern with the philosophical foundations of the social sciences, the eidetic characteristics of the life world—the third central element of *The Phenomenology of the Social World,* along with intentionality and sociality, which we have emphasized in our commentary on Schutz's position with regard to Husserl and Scheler.

Although Weber's essential concepts may have lacked full philosophical lucidity, as a sociologist, he had no need to integrate sociality within his conceptual framework. Here, he had the advantage over Scheler and Husserl. But Weber, in spite of his discovery of the subjective meaning of the actor; and Scheler and Husserl, in spite of their phenomenological comprehension of intentionality, all needed to be reminded of the uniqueness of the intended meaning of the Other. Thus, this brief historical survey unfolds for us the diverse strands that Schutz will weave together (essence, sociality, and intentionality), and it gives us a glimpse of Schutz's synthesis of sociology and philosophy in the making.

2
Meaning in a Social World

The Method of Schutz's Phenomenology

SCHUTZ'S *Phenomenology* reflects phenomenologically on the natural attitude from within that natural attitude. By undertaking his investigations from within the natural attitude, Schutz can accept the existence of the social world as it is always accepted in the natural attitude, whether in everyday life or in sociological investigation. As one commentator has noted, the major advantage of such a phenomenological psychology of mundane existence is that it can proceed within the horizon of intersubjectivity, whereas a transcendental phenomenology would of necessity place in brackets the existence of the Other and so would confront the problem of the constitution of the alter ego from the outset.[1] Hence, the restriction of his phenomenology to the level of phenomenological psychology permits Schutz, in the first place, to include human sociality— something that transcendental inquiry would methodologically exclude.[2]

If it is true that the naïve, taken-for-granted world is simply there, indubitable in the plausibility of its manifestness to all of us, then *Phenomenology*, which attempts to reflect on and express that givenness, to point out its shape and content, involves philosophic acts not on a par with mundane acts.[3] Thus, instead of taking objects of the social world as objects in themselves regarded as to what they are in truth and reality, Schutz's more reflective attitude withdraws from absorption in these objects themselves in order to consider the objects *as they are experienced* and the intentional structures through which they are given.[4] Schutz stakes out his own area of inquiry in Husserlian terms by affirming that "we now, as 'phenomenological psychologists' remain 'on the ground of inner appearance as the appearance of that which is peculiar to the psychic.'"[5] Schutz's uncovering of the meaning structures through which the social world is given to us entitles him to claim that his work is *phenomenological* in character. Disengaging such intentional structures from their anonymity forms the second main methodological component of Schutz's project in his *Phenomenology*.[6]

In the third place, Schutz does not concern himself with the empirical

34

facts of this inner sphere of appearance but rather seeks the invariant, unique meaning structures of the natural attitude and so conducts an inquiry into essence. Since such an eidetic examination involves a constitution of the object itself (here the entire natural attitude is the object) from the manifold of its concrete appearances, Schutz, again following Husserl, characterizes his own work as a *"constitutive* phenomenology of the natural attitude."[7]

Structure of Consciousness

On the basis of these three methodological stipulations, Schutz begins his phenomenology with a limited employment of phenomenological reduction in order to illuminate those intentional structures implicitly operative within the social world. This reduction involves changing one's attitude toward the natural attitude within which we live our day-to-day lives and wherein we accept the world given to us as being there. In the reduction, we (or, strictly speaking, I) place in abeyance belief in the existence of this outer world, neither denying its existence nor affirming it. Schutz insists that his analysis will be carried out within the phenomenological reduction only so far as it is necessary in order to acquire a clear understanding of internal time consciousness and, therefore, only within the second chapter of *Phenomenology,* "The Constitution of Meaningful Lived Experience in the Constitutor's Own Stream of Consciousness."[8]

Schutz first of all discovers the inner stream of *durée:* "A continuous coming-to-be and passing-away of heterogeneous qualities . . . In 'pure duration' there is not 'side-by-sideness,' no mutual externality of parts, and no divisibility, but only a continuous flux, a stream of conscious states."[9] This *durée* defines the limits of meaning, that backdrop of meaningless lived experiences against which reflection carves out meaning.

We apprehend the experience of this stream through four intentional structures that Husserl had explained: retention, reproduction, protention, and projection. Retention (primary remembrance), the after consciousness of the primal impression, is distinguished from reproduction (secondary remembrance), which, as reflective activity, introduces distinctions into experiences, differentiating them from one another and bringing discrete experiences into relief, thereby establishing meaning. Protentions consist of presentative orientations toward the future and differ from projection, the future-directed counterpart of reproduction, which represents, reflects in anticipation, and projects discrete events that will or might take place. For Schutz, our projective capacity to phantasize completed acts in the future toward which we will take certain necessary steps enables him to distinguish between action and behavior.[10]

The reflective act of reproduction establishes meaning, but it can only do so in relation to an experience previously unreflected on, lived through, not rendered discrete. Hence, the retrospective glance by which meaning is determined always occurs *after* the experience it singles out and endows with meaning. The beam of reflection can only be directed at experience from a later vantage point. The moment from which the ego reflects, the reflective act in which it lives, directed toward the elapsed and receding phases of the stream of *durée*, this moment itself is never captured in the cone of light directed retrospectively unless a further and later retrospective perspective is adopted on that reflective act of consciousness. In a sense, the act of reflecting itself remains on the horizon of the content on which it itself concentrates. Furthermore, we always undertake reflective activity from some particular moment, and the meaning of our lived experience will undergo modifications depending on the temporal distance from which we look back on it and remember it. An experience may take on a different meaning when reflected on three years after its occurrence than when reflected on immediately after its occurrence.[11]

But these reflective acts are not merely cognitive in nature; they are rather acts of attention, also described by Schutz as *attitudes* toward life. Schutz explicitly tells us that his attitudes bear a likeness to the emotive moods that Heidegger counts among the "existentialia of *Dasein*." This holistic epistemological theory, inseparably a theory of action and emotion, prevents any artificial separation of emotion and cognition and renders all reflective glances inevitably emotion and interest laden. Thus, both temporal and pragmatic determinations affect the reflective glance.[12]

Clearly, these temporally and pragmatically determined reflective acts will select certain experiences and endow them with meaning, leaving other experiences or levels of experience unattended. As Schutz notes, "Many of my experiences are never reflected upon and remain prephenomenal." Here, Schutz's analysis of consciousness resembles Dilthey's in which psychological cognition involves abstracting from the more comprehensive nexus of lived experience. Moreover, in contrast to Kant, who attributed to the subjective a priori the function of connecting originally separated given sensations, Schutz concurs with Scheler, whose subjective a priori does not create any synthesis, but selects, suppresses, disregards, and omits.[13]

According to Schutz, these reflective acts through which experience is given meaning depend on regularized schemes or categories that Schutz calls "typifications," which are built up through experience. In agreement with Husserl, Schutz claims that

in the natural attitude things in the factual world are from the outset experienced as types, namely, as trees, animals, snakes, birds, and in particular, as fir, maple, dog, adder, swallow, sparrow, etc. That which is apperceived as a type recalls similar things in the past and is to that extent familiar. Moreover, what is typically apperceived carries along a horizon of possible further experiences in the form of a predelineation of typicality of still unexperienced but expected characteristics of the object. If we see a dog we anticipate immediately his future behavior, his typical way of eating, playing, running, jumping, etc.[14]

Of course, since we are still speaking within the phenomenological reduction, we cannot refer to real dogs, adders, or swallows but must limit ourselves to speaking of the meaning configurations discoverable within consciousness. Nor, likewise, can we at this point treat the major means by which these typifications are bequeathed to us, that is, the language transmitted to us from the historical-social world into which we are born and within which we grow up, since that world is still in brackets.[15]

Whatever types we employ to interpret experience will depend on our practical interests and the problem at hand. Hence, for instance, if I wish to warn a child about the dog across the street, the typification *dog* would suffice, but if the humane society called me and wanted a description of the animal foaming at the mouth and staggering down the street, I might have to use the more detailed typification *large-sized German shepherd*. This pragmatic conditioning of types justifies Schutz's following comment: "There is no such thing as a type pure and simple. All types are relational terms carrying, to borrow from mathematics, a subscript referring to the purpose for the sake of which the type has been formed."[16]

Furthermore, if the set of typifications we have developed and inherited (as we shall see when the reduction is dropped) is the means through which experience is given to us, such that we experience things in the factual world from the outset according to these typifications, then it would follow that these typifications exercise a filtering function on what can be experienced or noticed in any given situation. Because we have a certain set of typifications, certain objects or aspects of objects will stand out for us in any experience and certain other objects or aspects will go unnoticed. A set of typifications itself carries with it certain proclivities to notice, certain *interests*, if you will. Interests determine types, and types, in turn, determine interests.[17]

Not only do selective interests and types mutually determine each other, but even the very formation of types involves a selection of some data and a suppression of other data. For instance, when I encounter a dachshund, a German shepherd, and an Irish setter and subsume them all under the type *dog*, I am prescinding from those properties that render them unique, individual, and irreplaceable. Instead of looking on them as dog′, dog″, and dog‴, where the primes designate a distinct individual, I suppress the primes by subsuming them under the common type *dog*.[18]

To be sure, Schutz's theory of typification, in which concepts and selectivity are inseparably bound up with each other, coheres neatly with his holistic epistemology. Schutz, in fact, believed that his theory of typification, which intertwines interests with typifications, advanced beyond that in Husserl's published writings.[19]

In *Reflections on the Problem of Relevance*, Schutz classifies these interest structures, which he calls *relevance structures*. Schutz isolates three types of relevance, each interrelated and interactive with the other. *Topical relevance* is that relevance by virtue of which something is constituted as problematic within an unstructurized field of unproblematic familiarity. Within the domain of *topical relevance*, Schutz distinguishes between those experiences that we make thematic by a volitive act and find implicitly offered in a paramount theme *(intrinsic relevances)* and those in which the division of a field into theme and horizon is imposed without our volition *(imposed relevances)*. In *interpretive relevance*, an aspect of present or previous experiences takes on importance for interpreting a new set of perceptions. *Motivational relevance* indicates the future goals or previous determinisms influencing an agent. The latter type of relevance, valuable for our study, includes in-order-to motives in which teleological goals attract us from the future, as it were, and because motives, which consist in those historical or environmental conditions that act on us from the past.[20]

This dual system of motives involves a complex, dual time sequence. In adopting an in-order-to motive, the actor projects into the future an act already completed in phantasy prior to taking any steps toward its realization. From the present, then, and on the basis of his whole past experience of how projects similar to this one have turned out, he looks forward to what *will have occurred* should he adopt this completed-in-phantasy act as his in-order-to motive and undertake the appropriate steps for its realization. He projects the act into the *future perfect tense*. On the other hand, for an actor or an Other to determine the because motive of an act, the act must first of all be already terminated. Then, from the present, whoever seeks to determine the because motive will be searching for a set of circumstances or events that existed *before* the past act and causally determined it. Hence, the because-motive investigator will seek events in the *pluperfect tense*, events that *had occurred* before the past event and influenced that past event's existence. The meaning context of the because motive is thus always an explanation after the event, constituted in a backward glance. Notice that what we construe to be the because motive, or, for that matter, what we project as an in-order-to motive, will essentially depend on relevances and typifications at hand at the present moment from which the past is being reflected on or the future anticipated.[21]

The relevances of any consciousness combine with other relevances in a system of relevances, as do typifications. Our types and the relevances correlative to them constitute a more or less consistent network that Schutz calls our stock of knowledge. Often, these accumulated and ordered components of our stock of knowledge—built up over time and so referred to as sedimented by Schutz—become so familiar to us that we remain oblivious to the previous conscious activity by which they were sedimented. Further, they are so habitually and successfully used and applied to experience that we take for granted how or in what polythetic acts they were originally constituted. This stock of knowledge includes such things as our awareness of the spatiotemporal conditions of any experience (for example, that I cannot be in two places at the same time); the fundamental structures of consciousness articulated in this chapter (for example, typifications and relevances); assorted skills (for example, walking); habitual or useful knowledge (for example, writing); knowledge of recipes for action (for example, the ability to read animal tracks); and fields of specialized knowledge (for example, a grasp of the methods and concepts of phenomenology). Depending on our interests and desires, there are manifold degrees of clarity and distinctness in our stock of knowledge, whole areas closed off to questioning, incompatibilities of which we are unaware, beliefs held with varying degrees of credibility, and areas of expertise and utter ignorance.[22]

Schutz further develops this polymorphic character of consciousness by demarcating various finite provinces of meaning, such as the everyday life world, the world of dreams, the world of science, the world of art, and the world of religious experience, each with their particular styles of lived experience, cognitive modes, and tensions of consciousness. As we shall see, the contours of our stock of knowledge and a social group's *social* stock of knowledge will aid in discussing the distribution of knowledge. However, now, because we are still abiding by phenomenological reduction, we cannot refer to an existent social group nor to those social and economic conditions that are, in great part, responsible for transmitting and shaping the different stocks of knowledge of individuals or groups.[23]

Intersubjective Understanding and the Structure of the Social World

Having explored the meaning structures of consciousness, Schutz discusses intersubjective understanding within the social world. At the beginning of his third chapter, "Foundations of a Theory of Intersubjective Understanding," he assumes the existence of the social world as we

assume it in the daily life of the natural attitude and in the social
sciences; that is, he assumes his own existence and that of the Other. In
so doing, Schutz has abandoned the strict method of operating under
phenomenological reduction, but he will still limit his focus to the meaning structures through which individuals build up a social world.[24] This
restriction conforms with his plan to construct a phenomenological
psychology "on the ground of inner appearance as the appearance of
what is peculiar to the psychic."[25]

The very positing of an Other with a stream of consciousness similar
to mine, though, immediately carries with it an important philosophical
implication that follows from Schutz's previous treatment of consciousness: Each individual consciousness is radically individualized
from every Other by its own unique history.

> The postulate, therefore, that I can observe the subjective experience
> of another person precisely as he does is absurd. For it presupposes
> that I myself have lived through all the conscious states and intentional
> Acts wherein this experience has been constituted. But this could only
> happen within my own experience and in my own Acts of attention to
> my experience. And this experience of mine would then have to
> duplicate his experience down to the smallest details, including im-
> pressions, their surrounding areas of protention and retention, reflec-
> tive Acts, phantasies, etc. But there is more to come: I should have had
> to live through these experiences in the same order that he did; and
> finally I should have had to give them exactly the same degree of
> attention that he did. In short, my stream of consciousness would have
> to coincide with the other person's, which is the same as saying that I
> should have to *be* the other person . . . "Intended meaning" is there-
> fore essentially subjective and is in principle confined to the self-
> interpretation of the person who lives through the experience to be
> interpreted. Constituted as it is within the unique stream of con-
> sciousness of each individual, *it is essentially inaccessible to every other
> individual.*[26]

In the light of the radical individuality of the Other and the detailed-
ness that a complete understanding of the Other would require, Schutz
concluded even from his Bergsonian period onward that there was a
necessary incommensurability between the meaning intended by one
person and the meaning understood by another.[27]

> It follows that the (subjective) meaning of my experience (which I, as
> objective meaning, hypostatize as the subjective meaning of your expe-
> rience) is always the meaning meant by me but never the meaning as
> understood by you. Thus, a discrepancy results between meaning
> intended and meaning understood, meaning posited and meaning
> interpreted. Or, as one says since Max Weber's basic investigations,

between objective and subjective meaning, a formulation which unfortunately has been often misunderstood.[28]

Schutz's theory of consciousness, then, leads him to an acute perception of differences between individuals that establish from the beginning the *limits* for any intersubjective exchange of meanings. It is interesting that at the very moment when Schutz adjusts his methodology to include the social world, which Husserl and Scheler never adequately accommodated within their theories, Schutz also brings into focus the radical uniqueness of each individual, which Scheler, Husserl, and Weber tended to disregard. For Schutz, we indeed resemble Leibnizian monads whose uniquely unfolding histories make it always questionable whether our perspective of the world actually harmonizes with the Other's.[29]

Although Schutz, unlike Leibniz, cannot resort to the metaphysical postulate of the deity to harmonize meanings, he does assure us that it is not impossible to understand another person's lived experience.

> We are asserting neither that your lived experiences remain in principle inaccessible to me nor that they are meaningless to me. Rather, the point is that the meaning I give to your experiences cannot be precisely the same as the meaning you give to them when you proceed to interpret them.[30]

The intended meaning of the Other thus functions as a limiting concept that I might approximate.

But the ordinary man living in the natural attitude does not appreciate these limits to interpersonal understanding in the same way that philosophers, such as Schutz, do. Rather, the ordinary man commonly calls a halt to the process of understanding other people's meaning when he has satisfied his practical concerns. He ignores the degree of misunderstanding present in social relationships as long as these relationships proceed satisfactorily according to his purposes.[31]

In Schutz's works after *Phenomenology*, he explains more fully how man in the natural attitude overcomes discontinuities between people and limitations to understanding the Other. Schutz argues that in the natural attitude, we implicitly accept two fundamental axioms: the existence of conscious fellowmen and secondly, the experienceability (in principle, similar to mine) by these fellowmen of objects in the life world. To be sure, various other stratifications of the life world (for example, space, time, personal history), known and taken for granted in the natural attitude, might modify just how similarly experienceable these objects are, but these modifications, which might affect only the second axiom, are set aside through the following idealizations implicitly employed in the natural attitude: the interchangeability of standpoints and the congruence of relevance systems.[32]

Interchangeability of standpoints signifies the taken-for-granted supposition that if I changed places with my fellowman, his here would
become mine, and I would be at the same distance from things and
would see them with the same typicality as he does and that the same
things would be within my reach that are within his. By the congruence
of relevance systems, Schutz means that until counterevidence surfaces
actors in the natural world assume that differences in their biographical
situations are irrelevant for dealing with common objects and one another as far as practical purposes are concerned. Both these idealizations
together constitute what Schutz terms the *general thesis of the reciprocity of
perspectives.*[33]

After treating these limits to understanding the Other and the mechanisms employed by man in the natural attitude to cope practically with
these limits, Schutz goes on to construct a theory of interpersonal understanding, or interpersonal *Verstehen*. This theory, explaining how we take
account of the meaning of the Other, relies on, of course, Schutz's
account of consciousness in which human actors give meaning to their
own experience by interpreting it through typified intentional structures. For Schutz, to grasp the meaning of anything entails interpreting
it according to the typicality of our prior experiences.

> The solution to this question [what it is for an object to enter our
> thematic field] is the new task the man must perform in order *to grasp
> the meaning of what is now within the thematic kernel of his conceptual field.*
> He must interpret it; and that means he has to subsume it, as to its
> typicality, under the various typical prior experiences which constitute
> his actual stock of knowledge at hand.[34]

Schutz thus locates interpersonal *Verstehen* within his broader theory of
meaning and understanding. Hence, in the natural attitude, for instance, we interpret our own lived experiences of the world, whether
these experiences be of inanimate things, animals, or human beings, by
subsuming them under previously acquired categories or typification
structures. As interpretive activity, all these interpretations can be classi-
fied as a first kind of *Verstehen*. According to Schutz, the interpreter can
interpret changes in the body of an Other in the same way he interprets
changes in inanimate objects, bestowing meaning within the sphere of
his solitary consciousness without taking into regard the consciousness of
the Other. However, he transcends this sphere only when these perceived changes in the Other's body come to be regarded as lived experiences belonging to another consciousness.[35] Here, in this second form of
Verstehen, we can only approximate the intended meaning of the Other,
since the limits mentioned above inevitably reassert themselves. Thirdly,
social scientists use a scientifically disciplined form of *Verstehen*. But for

Schutz, *Verstehen* is not primarily scientific. Rather, it is most basically the particular experiential form in which common sense thinking takes cognizance of the sociocultural world.[36]

Schutz presents a careful discussion of that basic type of *Verstehen* in which we interpret the actions of the Other as manifestations of another consciousness. In some cases, actors act without any communicative intent, and we, the interpreters, adopt the role of observers only, as for example, when we come across someone cutting wood who is unaware of our presence. Here, we would be prone to all the possibilities of misunderstanding that confront observers who cannot question the actor about the meaning his action has for him. Also, in the communicative context itself, some behavior occurs beyond the actor's control and without any intention on his part to communicate anything. These *expressive movements*, such as unwitting gestures or facial expressions, which are present in any conversation, betray conscious processes hidden from the actor himself.[37] In contrast to these expressive movements, there are also *expressive acts*, which proceed from a deliberate intention to communicate and may use a *sign system*. Schutz defines a sign system as a "meaning context which is formed by interpretive schemes; the sign user or the sign interpreter places the sign within this context of meaning."[38]

Even the simplest conversation involves a complicated network of expressive acts and corresponding interpretations. The interpreter, or listener, drawing on his personal knowledge of the speaker, tries to imagine the subjective meanings and purposes the speaker must have had in mind by making such a statement. Likewise, the speaker attempts to communicate his subjective meanings through speech skills he has acquired, but also drawing on his knowledge of his listener, he tries to communicate in such a way that he will be understood and accepted in accord with his listener's interpretive framework. In conversation, not only do we rely on our own expressive and interpretive contexts of meanings, but we also try to grasp the schemes of our partner and shape our expressions or interpretations in conformity with those schemes. Usually, when we listen to the Other or formulate a statement for him, we attempt to anticipate the meaning he will give to that statement.[39] Charles Horton Cooley dubbed this interlocking of glances, orienting ourselves by the supposed orientation of the Other to us, the *mirroring effect*.[40]

The signs with which sign users and sign interpreters operate can have objective, subjective, or occasional meanings. A sign has an *objective meaning* when it can be intelligibly coordinated to what it designates within a sign system independently of the one using the sign or interpreting it. In addition, a sign carries a *subjective meaning* that consists in the associations accruing to the sign from the unique quality of the experiences in which the sign user or sign interpreter learned to use the sign and his whole history of experience with that sign. This added meaning creates a kind of aura surrounding the nucleus of objective meaning. Further, the context in which a sign is employed, the surrounding words and circumstances of its use, also adds nuances to the objective meaning by giving it an *occasional meaning*.[41]

According to Schutz, the only way we might arrive at an objective meaning is by abstracting from a subjective meaning context. By a unique, selective act of attention, we can treat the movement of the Other's body, including speech acts or artifacts the Other has deposited, as products independent of their maker, focusing on the universal meaning of these objectifications and overlooking their author and everything personal about him. In this manner, we abstract objective meanings from the subjective, occasional contexts in which they are embedded. Further underscoring the derived character of objective meanings, we might ask whether the effort to express ourself in the objective categories of an available sign system necessarily leads to falsifying the author's subjective meaning.

> It should be noted that the fact of translating subjective knowledge into quasi-ideal and anonymous categories of meaning in a system of signs necessarily has as its consequence a "falsification" of this knowledge. The polythetical construction inherent in the acquisition of knowledge and the specific temporal dimension of subjective knowledge are "overcome." The alternatives and blind alleys of the acquisition fall away. The unique biographical constellation of the subjective meaning-structures in which the subjective elements of knowledge are embedded are bracketed out. The subjective meaning-contexts are largely replaced by the "Objective" meaning-context pertaining to the system of signs. The latter belongs, however, to a historical-social level of reality which transcends the individual (the one who posits the signs and the one who interprets them) . . .
>
> As a consequence of its translation in an anonymous system of signs, subjective knowledge itself is rendered anonymous.[42]

These remarks on the derivative nature of objective meanings can lead to such misinterpretations of Schutz as that by Habermas. He argues that both Schutz and Husserl ground linguistic symbols in the comprehensive appresentation achievement of the transcendental I. According to Habermas, for Husserl and Schutz, the monads spin linguistic intersubjectivity from themselves. Speech is not yet seen by them as the web on whose threads subjects depend and on which they first develop into subjects.[43] While Habermas's remarks may spring in part from Schutz's comments on the derivation of objective meanings, they also indicate that Habermas has not adequately distinguished between Husserl and

Schutz. Habermas seems to have overlooked Schutz's methological inclusion of the social by turning from transcendental to mundane phenomenology. Schutz, in a comment that would tend to confirm Habermas's convictions on the origin of linguistic intersubjectivity, makes evident the importance of his methodological strategy:

> [Intersubjectivity] is the fundamental ontological category of human existence in the world and therefore of all philosophical anthropology. As long as man is born of woman, intersubjectivity and the we-relationship will be the foundation for all other categories of human existence. The possibility of reflection on the self, discovery of the ego, capacity for performing any epoché, and the possibility of all communication and establishing a communicative surrounding world as well, are founded on the primal experience of the we-relationship.[44]

Furthermore, for Schutz, these socially induced capacities are developmentally acquired.

> To a large extent, the selection of the material which at any given moment of time becomes interpretationally relevant is a result of learning. As early as in childhood we have to learn what we have to pay attention to and what we have to bring in connection, so as to define the world and our situation within it. The selection and application of interpretationally relevant material, even after it is once learned, and has become a habitual possession and a matter of routine, still remains biographically, culturally, and socially conditioned. The same lifeworld lends itself to a magic interpretation by primitive people, a theological one by the missionary, and a scientific one by the technologist.[45]

Hence, earlier statements about the derivation of objective meanings from subjective-occasional contexts do not imply that there is no objective set of meanings in handed-down language systems, which, as a cultural deposit, antedate us and into which we must be initiated. Schutz is arguing rather that in any intersubjective encounter in the natural attitude two people will be able to agree on only an objective meaning of their terms by prescinding from the subjective and occasional meanings those terms have taken on due to their history, social conditioning, and present situation.

Similarly, the assertion that we distort our subjective meanings by resorting to an objective sign system might wrongly suggest that the subjective meanings that we experience within the stream of consciousness are somehow or other free from all those objective categories that constitute the external, social heritage of language. Rather, Schutz knows very well that we interpret our stream of consciousness through objective categories inherited from our social-historical environs, but these objective meanings become subjectivized, too, by being absorbed within our unique streams of consciousness with their unique histories and unique sets of social determinisms. These subject-objective aspects of language form part of a larger particular-universal relationship in evidence, for instance, in each individual's unique manner of taking on socially determined roles.[46] These tensions within Schutz's theory of language, which escape Habermas's notice, reflect Schutz's own synthesis of individuality and sociality, a synthesis Husserl and Schutz's other predecessors fell short of achieving.

The possibilities, though, that an interpreter can objectivate meanings by detaching them from their subjective-occasional setting or that subjective meanings can conceal themselves in the anonymous sign systems through which they reveal themselves render the process of intersubjective *Verstehen* all the more precarious. The process of *Verstehen* never overleaps the limits Schutz prescribes for it. The interpreter never comprehends the subjective meaning of the Other in its totality. This limit itself results from Schutz's theory of consciousness in which the intricacies of the Other's stream of consciousness always elude the interpreter's inevitably selective (because rooted in his *own* unique stream) intentionalities through which the Other is given to him.

After Schutz clarifies these limits of *Verstehen* and the different types of *Verstehen* functioning within the horizons of these limits, he proceeds to describe the different structures in which we experience social reality in the life world. First of all, there are immediate social relationships. In these, we turn our attention to the Other who shares our space and time and whose body offers a perceivable, explicable field of expression. This tuning in on the Other present, or *"thou orientation,"* can be unilateral or reciprocal. If it is reciprocal, a *we relationship* exists. In such a relation, we have access to the Other in a manner that he does not have to himself.

> As I watch his face and his gestures and listen to the tone of his voice, I become aware of much more than what he is deliberately trying to communicate to me. My observations keep pace with each moment of his stream of consciousness as it transpires. The result is that I am incomparably better attuned to him than I am to myself. I may indeed be more aware of my own past (to the extent that the latter can be captured in retrospect) than I am of my partner's. Yet I have never been face to face with myself as I am with him now; hence I have never caught myself in the act of actually living through an experience.[47]

I live through a we relationship rather than reflectively grasp it, but even so, whole sets of typified expectations and memories (of this or similar relationships), protentions and retentions (all bearing the mark of my own stream of consciousness) play themselves out in this immediate relationship. Here, I can easily and rapidly revise my typifications, and the more intimate and thorough my relationship with a person, the more confidence I usually place in my typifications of him.[48]

Immediate relationships, however, can devolve into mediate ones.

> I find myself face to face with an acquaintance. He excuses himself, shakes my hand, and departs. He turns around and calls out something to me. He is still farther, waves to me once more, and disappears around the corner. It would be difficult, if at all meaningful, to determine exactly when the we-relation came to an end, when the fellow-man who was given to me in immediate experience became simply a contemporary . . . A qualitative change in my experience of him has entered in, no matter when one would want to fix its point in time.[49]

In such mediate relationships, we adopt a *they orientation* in which the existence of the Other is not given to us (as in the we relationship) and in its place we construct a hypothetical personal type of the Other, a point of reference where all his personal characteristics as they existed when he departed intersect. In this case, when I write this Other, think of him, plan to go on vacation with him, I center my attention on this phantasized conjunction of personal characteristics. Naturally, such a type abstracts from the fullness of the individuality of the Other. It remains invariant unless I receive some evidence that he may have changed, and although I know he must be growing older, I tend to leave this out of consideration in the natural attitude, fixing the Other as he was when our we relationship broke off. This kind of *they relationship* involves relating to and acting from a distance on a partner who is an ideal construct of my own through typification constellations that are much less rapidly revisable than those in the we relationship. Finally, since I alter my typifications on only the basis of letters or reports of others who have seen him, my knowledge of the Other in this case becomes inferential and discursive rather than experiential.[50]

In addition to forming they relationships with someone who shares my time but not my space, and whom Schutz technically refers to as a *contemporary,* I can also enter into relationships with *predecessors* who, strictly defined, lived in the past and not one of whose experiences overlaps in time with one of mine. Since their life is complete, I can do nothing to change them, but they can still have an impact on me (for example, through a will). Here again, I must relate to these predecessors through a personal type, but the meaning contexts of their historical world may diverge so decisively from mine that my hold on their subjective meaning (for example, through documents or artifacts) is even less certain than my grasp of the subjective meanings of contemporaries, who at least share my same temporal perspective. Often, by means of the reciprocity of perspectives, the man of the natural attitude can pass over the troubling differences between his world and the world of predecessors, and he can assume that he understands them. Lastly, I can even form relationships with *successors* by imagining some hypothetical projected types of what characteristics they might have in the future.[51]

In the various strata in which social reality is experienced, the limits of *Verstehen* reappear. In the unreflective we relationship, I, the man of the natural attitude, am not often reflectively aware of differences between myself and my partner, but my interpretive schemata still bear the subscript of my unique stream of consciousness. Here, though, I can achieve better understanding than in the other strata, since I can more readily correct inaccurate typifications due to my immediate access to the Other and his expressive movements. But as I move farther away from the we relationship, into various forms of they relationships, the potential for not understanding increases, since all I really know is a construct of typical properties that substitutes for the bodily presence of the Other.

This condensed account of Schutz's phenomenology sets the stage for an explanation of the social distribution of knowledge, within which Schutz situates the sociology of knowledge. This phenomenology also provides the philosophical basis that sociology, eidetic phenomenology, and the sociology of knowledge take for granted. As such a basis for each of these areas, Schutz's phenomenology will help resolve difficulties and reassert often-forgotten limits.

3

The Distribution of Knowledge

ACCORDING TO SCHUTZ, the social distribution of knowledge provides the broad framework within which the traditional sociology of knowledge is located.

> Knowledge is socially distributed and the mechanism of this distribution can be made the subject matter of a sociological discipline. True, we have a so-called sociology of knowledge. Yet, with very few exceptions, the discipline thus misnamed has approached the problem of the social distribution of knowledge merely from the angle of the ideological foundation of truth in its dependence upon social and, especially, economic conditions, or from that of the social implications of education, or that of the social role of the man of knowledge. Not sociologists but economists and philosophers have studied some of the many other theoretical aspects of the problem. The economists discovered that certain concepts of economics, such as perfect competition and monopoly and all their intermediate forms, presuppose that the various actors in the world of economics are conceived as possessed of a varying stock of knowledge of the economic means, ends, procedures, chances, and risks involved in the same situation. Philosophers, in their turn, have dealt with the intersubjective character of knowledge, intersubjective not only because it refers to the one real world common to all of us and because it is subject to confirmation and refutation by others, but also because the personal knowledge of each of us refers to the knowledge acquired by others—our teachers and predecessors—and handed down to us as a preorganized stock of problems, with the means for their solution, procedural rules, and the like. All these manifold problems belong to a theoretical science dealing with the social distribution of knowledge.[1]

Schutz's use of the economic metaphor *distribution* in regard to knowledge and his reference to the varying amounts of knowledge present in conditions of perfect competition, monopoly, and their intermediate forms point to the influence of his friend Fritz Machlup. After Schutz's death in 1959, Machlup published *The Production and Distribution of Knowledge in the United States* and engaged in extensive empirical research into the distribution of knowledge. Machlup's work has dealt with how such factors as educational departmentalization, patents, communication media, newspapers, research allocations, information machines, censorship, and governmental classification of information allocate knowledge.[2]

Distribution possesses a quantitative significance insofar as it refers to variations in the *amount* of knowledge we have acquired. In addition, a qualitative configuration of knowledge results when diverse quantities of knowledge are brought together in a single stock of knowledge or when certain facts assume prominence and familiarity in our reserve of knowledge and others recede into the horizon of the irrelevant or unknown. Knowledge can be distributed within an individual's stock of knowledge, between two individuals in a personal relationship, or among various groups of a society. Both Schutz and Machlup understand *knowledge* in the widest sense of that term, from the grasp of remote theory to common-sense recipes for effective action, from knowledge *of* or *about* something to knowledge of *how* to do something.[3]

Three knowledge-distributing factors leave their mark on consciousness throughout Schutz's work: time, space, and social groups. Schutz himself concentrated on describing the meaning structures of consciousness in which these distributing factors become evident. He did not attempt to clarify the causal mechanisms through which these meaning structures were formed by, for example, trying to show how social groups impress themselves on individuals. Other philosophers, such as Scheler and Mead, have probed the causal origins of consciousness, and phenomenological findings can correlate with such causal investigations. Schutz, though, presupposes that these three factors have affected consciousness without trying to examine any causal links.[4]

The general structures of consciousness that Schutz articulates elucidate his conception of the distribution of knowledge. The typifications that we inherit or develop constitute our stock of knowledge at hand, our present knowledge distribution. These typifications, in turn, filter what knowledge we can or will acquire in any present or future experience. Furthermore, such typifications include not only the selective structuring mechanisms of perception and conception but also typical course of action patterns and roles.

> But it will be useful to remember that what the sociologist calls "system," "role," "status," "role expectations," "situation," and "institutionalization," is experienced by the individual actor on the social scene in entirely different terms. To him all the factors denoted by these concepts are elements of a network of typifications—typifications of human individuals, of their course-of-action patterns, of their motives and goals, or of the social-cultural products which originated in their actions. These types were formed in the main by others, his predeces-

sors or contemporaries, as appropriate tools for coming to terms with things and men, accepted as such by the group into which he was born. But there are also self-typifications: man typifies to a certain extent his own situation within the social world and the various relations he has to his fellow-men and cultural objects.[5]

It is clear, for instance, that a surgeon will collect certain information about his patient but be totally unconcerned about other facts pertaining to the patient. The surgeon's experience will over time also give him a vast store of information that someone who is not a surgeon will never share. Thus, the typified role behavior of being a surgeon corresponds to a particular distribution of knowledge that would not characterize a plumber, who, of course, has his own particular distribution of knowledge.

Relevances, intertwined with typifications in the stock of knowledge, also play a role in the composition of our present or future knowledge system. Whether we talk about the topic that is focal for us, the reserve of previous, remembered experiences interpretationally relevant to the situation at hand, or the motives at work—all these relevances determine what we now know and attend to and what we ignore or regard as of little interest, thus having a bearing on our distribution of knowledge. In addition, the imposed relevances of my situation, such as the crash of the automobile outside my window that interrupts my study and shifts the entire focus of my knowing or my need to make a living by doing factory work that leaves little time for reading, will affect the configuration of my knowledge at any one moment of time or throughout my whole life. Likewise, intrinsic relevances, such as my choice to explore the problem of sociology of knowledge and its ramifications instead of counterfactual statements, will distinguish my knowledge distribution from others'.

These types and relevances, organized more or less consistently in a stock of knowledge, a unique synthesis of knowledge with its own unexplored horizons, illustrate the qualitative and quantitative dimensions of the distribution of knowledge. For instance, a surgeon who has developed a taste for Rubens paintings might be attuned to aspects of such paintings that a nonaesthetic surgeon or a nonsurgical aesthete might overlook, but also, because of the time invested in developing his capacities, the surgeon might not know the least thing about the plight of the unemployed and their strategies to gain employment. Such divergences in personal stocks of knowledge explain why individuals can be characterized as expert in one or two areas of knowledge, relatively informed about others, and totally ignorant about some. These issues in the distribution of knowledge have been treated by Schutz through ideal-typical analysis in his essay "The Well-Informed Citizen" and by other sociologists under the auspices of the sociology of professions. Finally, our knowledge will be apportioned in a distinctive manner at any one moment of time or throughout our life depending on the province of meaning within which we predominately dwell, such as the religious, scientific, or aesthetic domains, or any combination of them.[6]

During this brief account of the distribution of knowledge in terms of Schutz's theory of consciousness, we have been implicitly referring to the three distributing factors of time, space, and social groups. For how else could we speak of how a surgeon's self-typified role organizes his distribution of knowledge without at least implying the *past* by which he built up a stock of surgical knowledge or the *future* in which he shall repeatedly formulate professional diagnoses that lead to successful interventions? How could we speak of the imposed relevance of a car crash outside my window without tacitly suggesting my spatial location that made hearing the crash and my resultant distraction and redistribution of relevances and knowledge possible? And how can we speak of a person playing the role of surgeon apart from the social system in which he is approved as a surgeon and acknowledged to be so by patients who play the role of patient in relation to him? These three factors require more detailed discussion.

The temporal structure of consciousness, of central importance to both Schutz and Husserl, conditions our distribution of knowledge. First of all, our stock of knowledge and shape of knowledge distribution within it is in continual temporal flux. Any supervening experience enlarges and enriches the fund of our knowledge. Merely having an experience gives us knowledge that we lacked prior to that experience. As Schutz points out, the same experience cannot be repeated because the second time we experience it, we have the added knowledge of having gone through it once before. The ordering of our knowledge is reshaped, albeit infinitesimally, by every increment in knowledge. The experiences we pass through also modify the modality of our beliefs. Things once held dubiously are confirmed when typified expectations are repeatedly borne out, or doubts are introduced when expectations explode. The character of our distribution of knowledge takes on different modal adumbrations throughout the temporal course of experience. Further, successive experiences also alter relevances and so in turn mold our distribution of knowledge.

> The emergence of a supervening experience results by necessity in a change, be it ever so small, of our prevailing interests and therewith of our system of relevances. It is this system of relevance, however, that determines the structurization of the stock of knowledge at hand, and divides it into zones of various degrees of clarity and distinctness. Any shift in the system of relevances dislocates these layers and redistributes our knowledge. Some elements that belonged previously to

the marginal zones enter the central domain of optimal clarity and distinctness; others are removed therefrom to the zones of increasing vagueness.[7]

Not only the temporal flux of experience but also the unity of our stream of consciousness, with the past, present, and future of our whole life intermeshing, serve to arrange our personal knowledge systems in diverse ways.[8] For instance, on the basis of our past knowledge, we interpret the present and design future projects that have reasonable prospects for success; hence, the extent and character of our knowledge of the present or the future will depend on our past accumulation of knowledge. Likewise, our past is interpreted in a certain light, and our future is anticipated on the basis of the dominant relevances and typifications in our present stock of knowledge.

Similarly, our knowledge of the future (in project form) will influence our knowledge of the past and present. Because of our knowledge of an adopted project, we shall, in turn, focus attention on certain related past experiences and the present means available for realizing our project. Also, on an intersubjective plane, only in the light of the knowledge of another actor's project can we ever hope to understand the present activity of this actor, the unity of his action, and his covert activities, such as refraining from action, failing to act, or refusing to choose. In addition, when we set out to realize a future project, acts often turn out differently than we had planned, unexpected data emerge, and projects may have to be repeatedly revised in the course of their realization. The final outcome of the project ends up not necessarily corresponding to the original plan. The scarcity of our knowledge about the future is gradually filled in as the future unfolds and our knowledge increases.[9]

Such contrasts in the sum of knowledge we command at different moments of our whole lives, the differing distributions of knowledge throughout our histories, underly the common experience that we wished we had known earlier in our lives what we have come to know later or that *now* we know what was going on in our lives *then* but only because the course of our history has illuminated the past for us. Finally, the continuity of our individual histories and the various experiences we have passed through, in their particular order and intensities, create a configuration of knowledge that belongs to us alone, which no Other can share, and which explains the heterogeneous distributions of knowledge to be found in the simplest dyadic human relationship.[10]

Our different temporal processes lead to differentiated distributions in the structure of the social world. It is possible, though, for two different temporal streams to share a common content of knowledge in we relationship while their two temporal sequences are overlapping.

The we relationship depends not only on spatial presence to each other but also on that sharing of time which Schutz calls *growing older together*. However, when a person introduces anonymity into a we relationship by placing himself at a spatial distance from the Other, the temporal structures of the relationship also undergo transformation. We "freeze" the Other as he was in the we relationship, even though we know very well that he must have changed through his new experiences—experiences, though, that are anonymous to us because we have not partaken in that temporal segment with him. In brief, the change in the temporal structure of the relationship diversifies the two distributions of knowledge.[11]

Schutz exemplifies these effects of time on the distribution of knowledge in his essay "The Homecomer." In that essay, differing distributions of knowledge ensue when a soldier withdraws from the spatiotemporal context of his family to carry on his own history overseas on the battlefront.

This is the aspect of the social structure of the home world for the man who lives in it. The aspect changes entirely for the man who has left home. To him life at home is no longer accessible in immediacy. He has stepped, so to speak, into another social dimension not covered by the system of coordinates used as the scheme of reference for life at home. No longer does he experience as a participant in a vivid present the many we-relations which form the texture of the home group. His leaving home has replaced these vivid experiences with memories, and these memories preserve merely what home life meant up to the moment he left it behind. The ongoing development has come to a standstill. What has been so far a series of *unique* constellations, formed by individual persons, relations, and groups, receives the character of mere *types;* and this typification entails, by necessity, a deformation of the underlying structure of relevances. To a certain degree the same holds good for those left behind. By cutting off the community of space and time, for example, the field within which the Other's expressions manifest themselves and are open to intepretation has been narrowed. The Other's personality is no longer accessible as a unit; it has been broken down into pieces. There is no longer the total experience of the beloved person, his gestures, his way of walking and speaking, of listening and doing things; what remains are recollections, a photograph, some handwritten lines. This situation of the separates persons is, to a certain degree, that of those in bereavement; "partir, c'est mourir un peu."[12]

In the light of these separated temporal currents and the resultant variations in knowledge complexes, the returning Homecomer is dismayed on his return: "When the soldier returns and starts to speak—if he starts to speak at all—he is bewildered to see that his listeners, even the sympathetic ones, do not understand the uniqueness of these individual experiences which have rendered him another man."[13]

Up to this point, particularly in the essay "The Homecomer," we have been presupposing that the temporal character of consciousness refers to the differing *internal times* of two separated streams of consciousness. Time also plays a distributing role in relation to knowledge by situating us in different moments of *objective time*, as it is measured by intersubjectively accepted calendars and clocks. Thus, in the example of the homecomer, both the family at home and the soldier at the front participate in the same objective time (for example, the days of the year, the passage of months), but their internal, subjective times vary radically.[14] Our location in objective time will make available and unavailable certain sums of knowledge. For example, it is possible that the twentieth-century Pentateuch scholar, because of recent archeological and literary-critical discoveries, might know more about the Pentateuch than his eighteenth-century counterpart, but both would know less than the Deuteronomist author.

The preceding example of the homecomer illuminates how knowledge-distributing factors, in this case temporal and spatial positions, are inextricably bound up with each other. Being in a different geographical location with different circumstances, events, and people recasts what the homecomer knows and how he knows it every bit as much as the fact that his ongoing history no longer coincides with that of his family at home.

This spatial determinant operates even in the most primitive of conscious acts, conditioning our distribution of knowledge in regard to the perceived object. For instance, as Husserl never tired of pointing out, any outer object cannot be grasped in its original selfhood but rather gives itself through a temporal series of presentations accessible from different spatial perspectives through which knowledge of an object is gradually built up. Hence, in the perceptual process, our knowledge is continually being increased and redistributed as new spatial perspectives correct or confirm earlier protentions or place past views in a new light. Therefore, our knowledge of the object will depend at any moment on, among other things, how many sides of the object have been seen, from what angle we are now viewing it, and how sharp our memory of the now invisible sides remains. Similarly, perceptual knowledge is distributed between two or more people, who from different angles of an object possess a distinctive awareness of that object. Although in such cases we may be unable to enter completely into the Other's perspective, by idealizing the reciprocity of perspectives, we can surmount to a degree this dispersion of knowledge by hearing the Other's report of how the object appears to him. We thereby gain access to aspects of reality not visible directly to ourselves and augment and redistribute our own knowledge. Further, our spatial position also accounts for the fact that contemporaries are no longer privy to the information about each other they held while they were in the we relationship, as we have seen. In fact, Schutz's discussion of the spatial distribution of knowledge in the structure of the social world can be seen as drawing out implications implicit in the Husserlian analysis of perception.[15]

Schutz's comments on letter exchanges between a soldier in combat and his family, an exchange between contemporaries, illustrate the very concrete and sad gaps in knowledge of the Other that can result from a change in physical location.

> To be sure, there still are means of communication, such as the letter. But the letter-writer addresses himself to the typification of addressee as he knew him when they separated, and the addressee reads the letter as written by the person typically the same as the one he left behind. Presupposing such a typicality (and any typicality) means assuming that what has been proved to be typical in the past will have a good chance to be typical in the future, or, in other words, that life will continue to be what is has been so far: the same things will remain relevant, the same degree of intimacy in personal relationships will prevail, etc. Yet by the mere change of surroundings, other things have become important for both, old experiences are re-evaluated; novel ones, inaccessible to the Other, have emerged in each partner's life. Many a soldier in the combat line is astonished to find letters from home lacking any understanding of his situation, because they underscore the relevance of things which are of no importance to him in his actual situation, although they would be the subject of many deliberations if he were at home and had to handle them.[16]

Space constitutes the second of three distributing factors.

Social affiliations define in part our distribution of knowledge, thereby affecting the *social* distribution of knowledge within which the so-called sociology of knowledge must find its place, according to Schutz. This third distributing factor does not function in isolation from space and time, since our spatiotemporal position places us in contact with determinative social groups. Moreover, in any social relationship, space and time portion out knowledge aggregates. For instance, the very meeting of two individuals with their own temporalities, their own past experiences in the particularity, sequence, and intensity in which they were experienced, unveils a distribution of knowledge in that relationship such that one partner would be able to grasp the intended meaning of the Other completely only if he were that Other. Similarly, knowledge is distributed in any we relationship by reason of the spatial location of the different interactors because each partner has access to the expressive field of the Other's body in a way that the Other does not. Hence, I can listen to the Other's voice tone or watch the Other's face and gestures and thereby observe those expressive movements that communicate information the Other is unaware of or even deliberately trying to conceal. But we must distinguish the distribution of knowledge *within* social relationships from the *social* distribution of knowledge, that distribution produced by belonging to social groups.[17]

For Schutz, the system of knowledge, that is, the interpretive meaning structures through which we apprehend the world, finds its origin in intersubjective communication.

> Any member born or reared within the group accepts the ready-made standardized scheme of the cultural pattern handed down to him by ancestors, teachers, and authorities as an unquestioned and unquestionable guide in all the situations which normally occur within the social world. The knowledge correlated to the cultural pattern carries its evidence in itself—or, rather, it is taken for granted in the absence of evidence to the contrary. It is a knowledge of trustworthy *recipes* for interpreting the social world and for handling things and men in order to obtain the best results in every situation with a minimum of effort by avoiding undesirable consequences . . . Thus it is the function of the cultural pattern to eliminate troublesome inquiries by offering ready-made directions for use, to replace truth hard to attain by comfortable truisms, and to substitute the self-explanatory for the questionable.[18]

A stranger to another culture discovers just how pervasive such cultural patterns of tested recipes are. He does not share the basic assumptions of that culture and so must learn through "his own bitter experiences of the limits of 'thinking as usual,' which has taught him that a man may lose his status, his rules of guidance, and even his history and that the normal way of life is always far less guaranteed than it seems."[19]

More specifically, there are cultural linguistic patterns that the in group shares, such as the fringe connotations of words, idioms, dialects, private codes, and the influence of literature, that an outsider does not have at his disposal. An erudite stranger, for instance, approaching an English-speaking country is heavily handicapped if he has not read the Bible or Shakespeare in the English language, even if he grew up with translations of those books in his mother tongue. Furthermore, although an in group member recognizes at a single glance the normal situations and apprehends immediately the ready-made recipe appropriate to them almost out of habituality, automatism, and half consciousness, a stranger must check tentatively every recipe for action he employs for its appropriateness. For example, a stranger is liable to treat aspects of typical functions as if they were individual; for instance, assuming that the milkman has a personal preference for a white suit and cap, or he is prone to take individual traits as typical; for example, expecting that all newspaper deliverers deliver at 4:30 A.M. These taken for granted, typified, linguistic, and behavioral patterns find their correlatives in higher level meaning structures, such as philosophical or theological idea systems by which an in group interprets itself and about whose relationship to underlying material factors (for example, race, geopolitical structure, political power relationships, conditions of economic production) sociologists of knowledge, such as Scheler and others, have discussed at length.[20]

Each in group constructs not only its own internal linguistic-behavioral practices and philosophical self-justifications, but also its interpretations of foreign groups. Such schemes of in group interpretation of the out-group refer to members of the foreign group as merely objects and beyond that, as neither addressees of possible acts emanating from interpretive procedures nor subjects of anticipated reactions toward those acts. Such knowledge of the other group is thus insulated and often not open to being verified or falsified by responses of members of foreign groups. Such interpretations of the out-group by the in group often involve a societywide mirroring effect. As an instance of such a looking-glass effect between social groups, Schutz cites a comment made by Justice Henry B. Brown in the 1896 U.S. Supreme Court case that defended separate but equal institutions for races. Brown opines regarding the Court's final act of decision:

> If inferiority is inferred from it, it is not by reason of anything found in the act but solely because the colored race chooses to put that construction upon it . . . Legislation is powerless to eradicate racial instincts . . . If one race be inferior to the other socially the Constitution of the United States could not put them on the same plane.[21]

Besides being, as Schutz notices, a poor attempt at justifying racial prejudice, this comment reveals Justice Brown already interpreting how the colored race will interpret his action. Schutz elaborates: "The imposition of social categories both creates the 'group' and invests it with a fictitious scheme of relevances that can be manipulated at will by the creator of the type."[22] In conclusion, our socially derived stock of knowledge, handed down by others, equips us with behavioral-linguistic patterns and higher level, self-interpretive meaning structures and categories with which to decipher other social groups and even their decipherment of us. Thus, the social groups to which we belong leave us a heritage of not necessarily accurate knowledge that varies from the distribution of knowledge inherited by a stranger or out-group member.[23]

Besides having knowledge transmitted to us from our past, we are compelled to derive knowledge from others in the present also, principally due to the limitations of our spatial position and the time available to us to research issues. So, according to Schutz, we rely on *eyewitnesses* who were there when I could be only here and whose relevance systems more or less conform with mine. Similarly, I depend on *insiders* who have better access but whose relevance systems diverge from mine or on *analysts* who arrange the knowledge they convey to me in accord with my perception of the situation and my relevances. Or I can make use of *commentators* who set data in order with a forthrightly acknowledged relevance scheme other than my own.

Knowledge is here distributed diversely because there are meaning-endowing subjectivities who have access to certain facts that they interpret through their own relevance-typification schemes, thereby putting that knowledge within reach of others. How these others will expand their own store of knowledge hinges on the reciprocity of perspectives by which they assume that if they were in the Other's position—spatial, temporal, or endowed with the same relevance system—they would see what he sees. This knowledge depends being sifted through the perspective of another and thus is socially derived and distributed.[24]

The previous examples suggest further that the social distribution of knowledge involves more than passing on a set of interpretive meaning structures. It also includes transmitting relevance systems, which is to be expected, given the interrelationship between typifications and relevances. Social groups convey relevances by reinforcing values, interests, emphases, and convictions about what is true or false, what is worth knowing or negligible. Thus, our own originary experiences, as well as any kind of socially derived knowledge, receive additional weight if they are also embraced by other members of our in group. I tend to believe my own experiences to be correct beyond doubt if others whom my social group considers competent corroborate them. As Schutz explains,

> If I consider my father, my priest, my government to be authoritative, then their opinions have special weight and this weight itself has the character of an imposed relevance. The power of socially approved knowledge is so extended that what the whole in-group approves— ways of thinking and acting, such as mores, folkways, habits—is simply taken for granted; it becomes an element of the relatively natural concept of the world, although the source of such knowledge remains entirely hidden in its anonymity.[25]

The socially approved character of knowledge contributes to various modalizations of the contents of our stock of knowledge (for example, it is held with certainty, high probability, dubiousness, depending on the degree of social reinforcement). Such modalizations are crucial to any description of the contours of our distribution of knowledge.[26] The social approbation of knowledge is intimately tied to that set of problems which Habermas and others address under the rubric of legitimation.[27]

An important qualification is called for, since we have spoken as though there were only *one* in group forming an individual's knowledge system. In fact, Schutz, following Georg Simmel, claims that our individuality is structured in accord with the numerous social groups to which we pertain and that pressure us from different directions.

> It must further be added that in the individual's definition of his private situation the various social roles originating in his multiple membership in numerous groups are experienced as a set of self-typifications which in turn are arranged in a particular private order of domains of relevances that is, of course, continuously in flux. It is possible that exactly those features of the individual's personality which are to him of the highest order of relevance are irrelevant from the point of view of any system of relevances taken for granted by the group of which he is a member. This may lead to conflicts within the personality, mainly originating in the endeavor to live up to the various expectations inhering in the individual's membership in various social groups . . . It is, however, at least one aspect of freedom of the individual that he may choose for himself with which part of his personality he wants to participate in group memberships; that he may define his situation within the role of which he is the incumbent; and that he may establish his own private order of relevances in which each of his memberships in various groups has its rank.[28]

Furthermore, our unique distribution of knowledge depends on the *history* of our participation in different social groups, the different weights with which those groups have impacted us, and the particular sequence in which we have been affiliated with them. The stages of our history of belonging to different social collectivities interact with each other such that membership in one group might dispose us to be more or less open to joining similar groups later in our history. Here again, the temporal structure of consciousness interacts with its social structure to distribute knowledge. The present status of our knowledge, while the product of previous social relationships, will both inform our intepretations of present and future social groups and institutions and also restrict or encourage the loyalty they will elicit from us.[29]

In conclusion, the notion of the distribution of knowledge is thoroughly consistent with Husserl's phenomenology. Knowledge distribution takes place through the fundamentals of his epistemology: internal time consciousness as flux and continuity, the spatiotemporal conditions of perception, and the constant modalization of knowledge. Husserlian phenomenology itself is synonymous with a distribution of knowledge by space and time.

Schutz, however, introduces a third distributing factor that Husserl was methodologically prevented from including: the social. By setting aside phenomenological reduction, Schutz allots a distributing role to "the social world as it is always accepted in the attitude of the natural standpoint, whether in everyday life or in sociological observation."[30] This social distribution of knowledge becomes evident in Schutz's theory of intersubjective *Verstehen* in which two individuals more or less understand each other in part by reason of the social groups to which they have been attached. Moreover, the social distribution comes to the fore in the structure of the social world in which consociates, contemporaries, predecessors, and successors command varying distributions of knowledge in regard to each other due to diverse social contexts from which they emerge. *Phenomenology* represents both an outcome and extension of the distribution of knowledge implicit in Husserl's descriptions of how knowledge accumulates and undergoes transformation as we walk around a house or encounter new data that modalizes prior beliefs.

The social distribution of knowledge follows inevitably from Schutz's effort to synthesize the social with Husserl's account of the intentional structures of consciousness. However, Schutz's inclusion of the social has not eliminated the distinctive intentionality of the Other, as the works of Scheler, Husserl, and Weber threatened to do. On the contrary, Schutz's incorporation of the social has simply added another dimension to the radical uniqueness of each individual, whose knowledge distribution differs from that of every Other's because his spatial position, history, and nexus of social affiliations are shared by no one else.

4

The Distribution of Knowledge as Protosociology

Schutz's Phenomenology: The Meeting Place and Foundation of Sociology and Philosophy

THE EIDETIC CHARACTER of Schutz's synthesis of intentionality and sociality enables his description of the life world to serve as a foundation for sociology and eidetic phenomenology. This eidetic quality of Schutz's work implies that any and every concrete, socially conditioned set of meaning structures, through which we interpret the world and our experience, will, *of essence,* consist in *some* arrangement of typifications and relevances within a stock of knowledge, or, in other words, *some* distribution of knowledge. On the one hand, it is necessary for any life world to have typifications, relevances, and stocks of knowledge and these must be spatiotemporally and socially derived. It is also contingent and empirically determinable what those typifications, relevances, and stocks of knowledge will concretely look like as we move from one empirical group to another.

Both social science and phenomenology, particularly eidetic phenomenology, adopt higher level reflective postures toward this life world, even though these often take that life world and its structures for granted. Schutz's portrayal of the universal features pertinent to all life worlds thus provides a philosophical foundation for phenomenology and sociology, a kind of protophilosophy or protosociology.

Schutz's criticism of the social sciences for failing to clarify the basic sociological phenomena they investigate shows that he envisioned his own work as protosociological.

> To give just one example, all social sciences take the intersubjectivity of thought and action for granted. That fellow-men exist, that men act upon men, that communication by symbols and signs is possible, that social groups and institutions, legal and economic systems and the like are integral elements of our life-world, that this life-world has its own history and its special relationship to time and space—all these are

notions that are explicitly or implicitly fundamental for the work of all social scientists. The latter have developed certain methodological devices—schemes of references, typologies, statistical methods—in order to deal with the phenomena suggested by these terms. But the phenomena themselves are merely taken for granted . . .

But how does it happen that mutual understanding and communication are possible at all? How is it possible that man accomplishes meaningful acts, purposively or habitually, that he is guided by ends to be attained and motivated by certain experiences? Do not the concepts of meaning, of motives, of ends, of acts, refer to a certain structure of consciousness, a certain arrangement of all the experiences in inner time, a certain type of sedimentation? And does not interpretation of the Other's meaning and of the meaning of his acts and the results of these acts presuppose a self-interpretation of the observer or partner? How can I, in my attitude as a man among other men or as a social scientist, find an approach to all this if not by recourse to a stock of pre-interpreted experiences built up by sedimentation within my own conscious life? And how can methods for interpreting the social inter-relationship be warranted if they are not based upon a careful description of the underlying assumptions and their implications?[1]

As a consequence of their lack of philosophical foundations, some of these social scientists (for example, behaviorists, such as Skinner) have tended to imitate the natural sciences in assuming that social reality could be discussed objectivistically, without inquiring into the subjective activities of mind out of which the life world is built up. Schutz, following Husserl's *Crisis*, traces this self-forgetfulness to the development of Galilean natural science, which, ignoring its own scientific attitude of mind, develops an abstract, scientific description of nature, stripped of all perceptual, affectual, or poetic attributes, and claims that this is how nature exists apart from any mental activity (since it ignores its own mental activity). Social scientists have mistakenly adopted this mentally pared-down construct of nature as the model for conceiving social mind. Thus, Schutz proposes to bring phenomenology to bear on the social sciences, to provide them with fundamental concepts, and to reestablish within them the rights of forgotten subjectivity.[2]

But, in phenomenology's attempt to meet sociology at its base, phenomenology must adapt itself to its task. Hence, Schutz rejects any phenomenological approach to the social sciences from within the transcendental sphere, since the conrete sciences of cultural phenomena relate to that mundane sphere that transcendental phenomenology has bracketed. In addition, Schutz takes exception to Husserl's comments on social groups, his personalization of collectivities, his constitution of the Other from within the transcendental sphere, and his unwarranted inferences and empathic transferences in regard to the experience of the

Other. Over and above this, Schutz criticizes Husserl's second *epoché* in the Fifth Cartesian Meditation by contending that not only the products of the sense determination of other subjectivities but also our consciousness of them are socially determined. In the same vein, Schutz objects to the problematic use of eidetic method by Edith Stein, Gerda Walther, and the early Scheler, all of whom arrived at hypostatized *Gesamtpersonen*.[3]

Schutz found Scheler, however, to have markedly improved when he later postulated as a prerequisite of any phenomenological reduction a theory of the nature of reality and our experiencing of it. Schutz agrees with Scheler that this general thesis of reality in the natural attitude and its anthropomorphic character is susceptible to phenomenological analysis. For Schutz, the *content* (but not the universal structures) of this relative natural attitude changes from group to group and within the same group throughout its historical evolution. The description of these varied contents is the responsibility of the empirical social sciences. Clearly, at this point, Schutz reads Scheler as approximating his own position in *Phenomenology*. That work does not consist in an account of any concrete, relative natural conception of the world of some particular group at some point in its history. Rather, it seeks the a priori structures to be found in *any* relative natural conception of the world. This eidetic character of Schutz's phenomenology permits him to establish a philosophical domain distinctive from that of the empirical sciences, which concentrate on the diverse empirical manifestations of these a priori structures. In sum, Schutz apparently considered his own thought as offering that philosophical anthropology prerequired for any theory of phenomenological reduction.[4]

In brief, Schutz as a phenomenologist was moving toward the social sciences in hopes of offering them a philosophical foundation that would clarify the phenomena they examine with assorted methodological devices but take for granted. Thereby, he also intended to allow scope for the subjective intentional structures that the naturalistically inclined social sciences were in danger of consigning to oblivion. At the same time, however, this turn toward the social sciences called for a reappraisal of phenomenology. Schutz's constitutive phenomenology of the natural attitude permitted the inclusion of the sociality Husserl methodologically bracketed, avoided the pitfalls of an ill-employed eidetic methodology, and resulted in the socialization of those meaning structures, those "consciousnesses of," whose social formation Husserl overlooked.[5] Schutz's effort to philosophize sociology led to a sociologization of philosophy.[6]

In providing, then, a conceptual undergirding for the social sciences and a philosophical anthropology as a prelude to phenomenological reduction and eidetic reflection, Schutz's work can rightfully claim the status of a protosociological philosophy. Schutz eidetically sets forth the structures of the mundane world, thus paving the way for the phenomenological *epoché*, always conceived by Schutz not as an entrance into a separate ontological realm, but as an attitude assumed toward the mundane world. We wonder if critics of Husserl, such as Derrida or Foucault, who fault Husserlian reduction for its inability to exclude social factors, might have been more favorably disposed if the reduction had been presented as an attitudinal mode of attending to a life-world base in which the social had already been given its full due. Schutz's constitutive phenomenology of the natural attitude affirms this social formation of typifications of consciousness on which the phenomenological reduction does not focus but which it definitely presupposes.[7]

Objectivity in Social Science: Weber and Nagle

A discussion of Schutz's meaning of social-scientific objectivity illuminates the protosociological nature of his phenomenology and the importance of his phenomenology for sociological investigation and, ultimately, for the sociology of knowledge. Objectivity in the social sciences depends on Schutz's delineation of objectivity in the natural attitude. In that natural attitude, we are so immersed in our acts directed toward their objects that our entire subjectivity can remain anonymous to itself. Thus, we assume that the objects we know are detached from, and independent of, anyone's definition of the situation and unique biographical circumstances. They are objectively and obviously there, and by what Schutz calls the *epoché* of the natural attitude, we suspend all doubt about the existence of this outer world and its objects and all doubt that the world and its objects might be otherwise than they appear to us.[8]

Schutz's more reflective scanning of the natural attitude, though, by bringing to light differences between individuals in the simplest encounter, undermines such naïve beliefs in objectivity. This disturbance of the natural-attitude faith shows up at the level of objective meanings of language. The historical and social distributions of knowledge, which individualize each subjectivity and condition its reception and production of objective word meanings in the simplest interchange, prompt Schutz's almost despairing observation, "In fact, we can even say that the understanding of the objective meaning is an unrealizable ideal."[9]

By the end of *Phenomenology*, Schutz settles for a definition of the objective meaning of an expression as that meaning received within the meaning context of the interpreter as opposed to the significance that expression has for the producer of the expression, its subjective mean-

ing. Here, objective meaning is not a meaning transcending any subjectivity but rather a meaning relative to that subjectivity standing as an
interpreter in contrast to another subjectivity expressing itself. "The
terminology is unfortunate because the term 'objective meaning' is obviously a misnomer, in so far as the so-called 'objective' interpretations
are, in turn, relative to the particular attitudes of the interpreters and,
therefore, in a certain sense, 'subjective.'"[10]

It is even possible for an interpreter to prescind completely from the
subjective meaning context giving birth to an expression of meaning and
consider the objective meaning of the product in itself apart from the
lived experience of its author.

> The objective meaning of a product that we have before us is, on the
> other hand, by no means interpreted as evidence for the particular
> lived experience of a particular Thou. Rather, it is interpreted as
> already constituted and established, abstracted from every subjective
> flow of experience and every subjective meaning-context that could
> exist in such a flow. It is grasped as an objectification endowed with
> "universal meaning." Even though we implicitly refer to its author
> when we call it a "product," still we leave this author and everything
> personal about him out of account when we are interpreting objective
> meaning . . . But precisely for this reason the objective meaning re-
> mains, from the point of view of the interpreter, invariant for all
> possible creators of the meaningful object. Insofar as that object con-
> tains within its very meaning the ideality of the "and so forth" and of
> the "I can do it again," to that extent is that meaning independent of its
> maker and the circumstances of its origination. The product is ab-
> stracted from every individual consciousness and indeed from every
> consciousness as such. Objective meaning is merely the interpreter's
> ordering of his experience of a product into the total context of his
> experience.[11]

This Schutzian explanation of natural-attitude objectivity lays the
ground for objectivity in the social sciences. Schutz's essay "Concept and
Theory Formation in the Social Sciences" includes two very different
meanings of social-scientific objectivity. The first, which we shall dub
Weberian, requires the social scientist to assume the role of interpreter of
subjective meanings of the Other. This interpreter's meanings will thus
be objective in the sense of the interpretive objectivity defined in *Phenomenology.*[12] However, social-scientific objectivity mandates implementing certain scientific procedures, which, as we shall see, the life-world
interpreter of the Other's meanings does not adopt. Nevertheless, the
objective meaning that the social scientist articulates must also refer to,
and take account of, the subjective meaning of the actor by reason of
Weber's postulate of subjective interpretation.[13]

The second meaning of objectivity in the social sciences corresponds to Ernest Nagel's insistence on the need for controlled verification and opposes any subjective arbitrariness in the pursuit of social science. Schutz concurs with Nagel: "I agreed with Professor Nagel's statement that the social sciences, like all empirical sciences, have to be objective in the sense that their propositions are subjected to controlled verification and must not refer to private uncontrollable experience."[14]

Schutz attempts to integrate both these kinds of objectivity and to sketch out procedures for their attainment in his essay "Concept and Theory Formation in the Social Sciences." Prior to doing this, he asks at the beginning of that essay the most serious question that the methodology of the social sciences must answer, namely, how is it possible to form objective concepts and an objectively verifiable theory of subjective meaning structures. In response, he asserts that the concepts formed by the social scientist are actually constructs of constructs formed in common-sense thinking by actors on the social scene.

In building up these second-level concepts in order to interpret subjective meanings of the life worldly Other, the social scientist adopts the attitude of a social-scientific observer to achieve Weberian objectivity. By assuming this scientific attitude and its correlative scientific procedures, the scientist can clarify those meanings accepted without criticism or held in a confused fashion in the nonreflective, lived experience of the life world. Schutz points out: "Every social science, including interpretive sociology, therefore, sets as its primary goal the greatest possible clarification of what is thought about the social world by those living in it."[15]

What then is this particular attitude distinguishing the scientific interpreter from the life-world interpreter of the Other's subjective meanings and enabling him to clarify what the Other in his lived experience takes for granted? First of all, the decision to carry on science involves a free choice, a leap reminiscent of Kierkegaard's leap of faith. This decision to pursue science involves changing our relevance system with regard to the natural attitude. Through scientific *epoché,* we exclude pragmatic interest in shaping the world and assume a passionate theoretical interest in observing and illuminating it. The social scientist, then, removes himself from his biographical situation within the social world, considers his relevances within the social world as irrelevant to his scientific undertaking, and detaches himself from the value patterns that govern or might govern actors on the social scene.[16]

Schutz also admits that the decision to "do science" is tied to a specific science, scientific problem, and depth of investigation. The choice to engage in scientific work also plunges us into a world that is preconstituted by the findings of others, their formulation of problems, and their projected methods and solutions. The theoretical world is a self-enclosed meaning world with its own style of achievements, its own problem complexes, and its own horizons of problems still in need of solution. The consideration of any problem depends on the collective cosmos of the scientific world that often restricts our freedom to frame a problem and potential for creativity.[17]

Schutz summarizes the qualities of the Weberian mode of objectivity that results from setting in place the scientific *epoché* and inserting ourselves within the scientific situation.

> The scientific problem, once established, alone determines what is relevant for the scientist as well as the conceptual frame of reference to be used by him. This and nothing else, it seems to me, is what Max Weber means when he postulates the objectivity of the social sciences, their detachment from value patterns which govern or might govern the behavior of the actors on the social scene.[18]

Once the social scientist has placed himself in the scientific situation, he observes those facts and events within social reality referring to human actions. His perspective, cut off from the lived we relationship and resembling that of the indirect social observer toward his contemporaries (although this observer has not embraced the scientific *epoché*), forces him to consider actions he observes in their typicality and not in their uniqueness. As a social scientist interested in clarifying regularities, he focuses on the typically relevant acts of actors proceeding from motives that are constant and invariant, that is, acts having a certain probability of repetition and frequency.[19] As a result, the social scientist constructs typical behavior or course-of-action patterns, which he then coordinates to model an ideal actor whom he imagines to be gifted with consciousness. Thus, enacting this scientific attitude and applying the soon-to-be-explained postulates ensure that concepts derived are objective in a social-scientific sense. At the same time, however, the very use of the personal ideal type, which takes into account the consciousness and subjective meanings of the life-world actor so typified, also captures subjective meaning structures, thereby satisfying Weber's postulate of subjective interpretation.[20]

How, though, does Schutz meet Nagel's criterion of objectivity? First of all, Schutz rejects the criterion of objectivity proposed by sensationistic empiricism, namely, that all claims be based on objective sensory observation, because it fails to deal adequately with the object of the social sciences. That object is the intersubjective life world and processes of mutual understanding and interpretation at work there that Schutz's constitutive phenomenology of the natural attitude eidetically delineates.

In fact, the community of social scientists assumes such processes of mutual understanding in their relations with each other. Phenomenology, which already takes as its subject matter the entire range of intentional activity, as one commentator has put it, is better suited than sensationistic empiricism to deal with this intersubjective life world and the interchange of interpretations between conscious subjects.[21]

Although Schutz disagrees with Nagel's criterion of objectivity, he emphatically concurs with Nagel that the propositions of the social sciences have to be subjected to control and must not refer to private, uncontrollable experience. Schutz's understanding of social science as constructing types of typical constructs employed on the common-sense level permits him to escape any charge that he is referring to private, uncontrollable experience. Scientific *Verstehen* depends on common-sense *Verstehen* by which actors in the life world take cognizance of their sociocultural world, assessing each other's intentions, and shaping their responses in accord with culturally defined and learned norms. Just as this common-sense *Verstehen* need not refer to private experiences accessible by introspection only, so scientific *Verstehen*, which investigates these processes of common-sense *Verstehen*, need not either.[22]

In order to secure control, or nonarbitrariness, for social-science propositions, Schutz specifies three postulates with which social scientists must comply in order to assure the objective verifiability of the types they construct. These typical constructs must be established with the highest degree of clarity and distinctness and be fully compatible with the principles of formal logic (postulate of logical consistency). Secondly, the scientific types must be referable to the subjective meaning that an action or result of an action had for the actor (postulate of subjective interpretation). Finally, each term in a scientific model of human action must be constructed in such a way that a life-world actor would find such an action understandable according to his common-sense interpretation of everyday life (postulate of adequacy). This last postulate recognizes that the distribution of knowledge possessed by the social scientist varies from that of the actor in the social world and obliges the social scientist to test the accuracy of his assessment of a situation against the life-world actor's reading of it.[23]

Schutz's phenomenology upsets the taken-for-granted objectivity characteristic of the natural attitude and eventually presents a new definition of natural-attitude objectivity as the meaning in the interpreter's mind as opposed to the meaning in the expresser's mind. Social-scientific objectivity, paralleling that of the natural attitude, comes to signify the particular attitude taken up within scientific *epoché* by a scientific interpreter of the subjective meanings of a life-world actor. A second kind of social-scientific objectivity refers to those results flowing from the public character of all *Verstehen,* including its scientific variant, and from observance of the three postulates.

The Limits of Social Science: The Horizonality of Consciousness and the Otherness of the Other

Our description of the scientific *epoché* by which Weberian objectivity is achieved, which transcribes German sources in the Schutz archive, involves some rather bold claims: "The social scientist . . . removes himself from his biographical situation within the social world, considers his relevances within the social world as irrelevant to his scientific undertaking, and detaches himself from the value patterns which govern or might govern the actors on the social scene."[24]

There are two ways of looking at this description of scientific *epoché.* First of all, Schutz could be seen as describing the scientific attitude and its relation to its object as they can be found in actual scientific practice. Secondly, the scientific attitude can be conceived as a normative principle whose force is to penetrate and guide other layers of consciousness.

According to the first interpretation, Schutz's description of the scientific attitude would begin with actual scientific experience. The practicing social scientist is well aware that certain lived experiences can emerge from obscurity and confusedness into a certain clarity through scientific reflection. The laws of economics, crystallized from lived economic exchanges, Schutz's own clarification of confused concepts in Weber, or his own phenomenological psychology, illuminating phenomena taken for granted in the social sciences, are cases in point.[25] The change in the status of the object from obscure to clear indicates the presence of a different noetic stance than lived absorption in the object—the noetic stance of the scientific attitude.

Schutz's complete description of scientific *epoché* offers a philosophical interpretation of that common scientific experience, and it develops fully the character of this new noetic standpoint. For Schutz, obscurities may be traced to the lived experience of the life world, which is the context for scientific *epoché,* analogous to phenomenological *epoché.* Like its phenomenological counterpart, scientific *epoché,* is nothing but the adoption of a certain reflective attitude, a certain attentional tension, toward the life world. Although the social scientist may not self-consciously execute this *epoché* with all the formality and detail that Schutz ascribes to it, nevertheless, as soon as he reflects on his and others' life-world experience, he has undergone a subtle shift in the tension of his consciousness. Such a shift often occurs so rapidly and subtly as to be almost unnoticeable.[26] Thus, the social scientist no longer lives in his experience; rather, he reflects on it and so engages in a primitive form of *epoché* anticipative of that *epoché* formally elaborated by Schutz.

By this shift in the tension of consciousness, the scientist no longer strives toward the goals to which lived experience is directed, since his new purpose (relevance) is to clarify that lived experience itself. Further, he is aware of his scientific community's questions about that experience, and he seeks answers to them, even though neither these questions nor answers concerned him while living in the experience. He has abandoned his biographical situation, altered his relevances, and detached himself from the value patterns of one living in the experience *in the sense* that he has turned toward these formerly lived-in experiences with a different attitude than living in, namely, that of reflecting on.[27]

In light of Schutz's description of scientific *epoché* as analogous to phenomenological *epoché*—which for Schutz means not transmigration into a different ontological realm but a shift in attitude[28]—we can avoid misunderstandings possible from a superficial reading of the seemingly bold claim with which we began. First of all, Schutz is not claiming that the life-world experience, biographical situations in the social world, life-world relevances, and values governing actors on the social scene are to be disregarded as if they were objects unimportant to social science— exactly the opposite. In fact, Schutz insists, in complete consistency with his postulate of adequacy, that while scientific types are being constructed, "there must be constant recourse to pregiven knowledge of the social world and of the world in general."[29] These lived experience of ourselves and others are of utter importance, but as the *objects* of reflection, as having-been-lived-through experiences that are "seen through" by a later sociological reflective attitude. Secondly, if the social scientist's life-world relevances resemble or are in sympathy with those of a life-world actor, then those life-world relevances offer potent sources from which the social scientist's reflective attitude may benefit. But for Schutz, such biographical elements are to be available through a different attitudinal focus than that of living within them.[30]

This first account of Schutz's depiction of scientific *epoché* construes it as an effort to explain philosophically how social science renders transparent confused, lived experiences. The clarity of the object corresponds to a change in noetic attitude whose purpose is clarification in cooperation with a community of scientists. This reflective attitude requires no metaphysical departure from the life world, no disregard of life-world realities, nor suppression of sensitivities cultivated within the life world.

Schutz's description of scientific *epoché* also *prescribes* how the social scientist *ought* to proceed. This second interpretation of scientific *epoché* conceives it as calling for a frame of mind that *ought* to govern all the manifold layers of consciousness. The life-world relevances that the previous interpretation confined to the status of an object focused on by a reflective attitude also pervade the subject who undertakes that reflective attitude. This second view of scientific *epoché* calls for subordinating these relevances to the scientist's reflective goals. But how possible is it to complete such a subordination or to know that it has been completed? To answer this question and thus determine the feasibility of implementing the scientific *epoché* under this prescriptive interpretation of it, we do not begin with the object and the attitude correlative to it as disclosed within actual scientific practice. Rather, we turn to the analysis of consciousness itself.

For Shutz, the temporal structure of the reflective act itself makes any inspection of that act and the relevances determining it impossible *while that act itself is taking place.* Only a later act of reflection can capture and indicate the contours of a present reflective act. Hence, part of the horizon of any reflective act is the act itself and the relevances determining it.[31] Thus, it would not be possible to reflect and certify *at the same* time that our reflecting remains free of relevances distorting our speculative outcomes. Only a later act of reflection would be capable of guaranteeing the objectivity of an earlier act, but, of course, that later reflective act cannot guarantee its own freedom from bias while it is being lived out. Our colleagues can aid in this process of criticism, but how can they ensure that their lived acts of reflection are free from communal prejudices except by later reflective acts equally vulnerable to subsequent critique? The procedures by which we certify objectivity— retrospectively scrutinizing earlier acts in which we were so occupied with another focus that we could not be self-critical or submitting our work to the review of colleagues who might see what we have been unable to see ourselves—these procedures form a part of the problem of the distribution of knowledge. Such procedures will always be necessary as long as our knowledge configuration depends on our temporal position, thematic relevances, and social commitments.

Shutz's account of reflection and its horizons resembles Merleau-Ponty's conviction that the reflective act of phenomenological reduction illuminates precisely those horizons of consciousness that render the very project of reduction, namely, refraining from all existence valuations, impossible to complete. The nature of reflection itself raises the question whether we can ever guarantee with certainty that we have fully satisfied the scientific *epoché's* demand to master consciously and withdraw entirely from those life-world evaluations and inclinations forming the backdrop of scientific reflection. Can the scientific *epoché* be any more capable of completion than its phenomenological analogue?[32]

In summary, we can construe scientific *epoché* according to Shutz by two different readings. The first admirably delineates the nature of the scientific attitude at its best, bringing to reflective lucidity what was formerly opaque in its livedness and fulfilling Weber's injunction for objectivity in the social sciences. The second, though, displays the boundaries within which that reflection and the quest for scientific objectivity labor. Reflection, precisely by thematizing, marginalizes what remains unthematic to a horizon, including its own motivations. This dual-faced nature of reflexivity and *epoché*, also apparent in critical discussions of phenomenological *epoché*, becomes manifest in Schutz's account of the primitive act of reflection, whose very illumination of the experiences of stream of consciousness leaves in its wake a manifold of the unexamined.

Just as the horizonal theory of consciousness delineates the scientific attitude and the objectivity it targets, so also *Phenomenology*, while providing a basis from which both the Weberian and Nagelian theories of objectivity arise, establishes their limits.

Schutz has incisively seen that in order to do sociology we must enter into an interpretive relationship with the life-world actor, even though it be something like a relationship between contemporaries, only one of whom has instituted scientific *epoché*.[33] The Weberian sociologist must interpret the meanings of the Other, and he can misinterpret those meanings as easily as any life-world interpreter can. We, as sociologists, can never understand the meanings of the Other as the Other understands them by reason of the different historical and social circumstances through which we and the Other have passed and that have resulted in our varied distributions of knowledge. The Other's meanings remain as much a limit concept for the scientific interpreter as for his life-world counterpart.

Further, the scientific interpreter, by reason of distance from the Other that his scientific methodology imposes on him, attempts to understand the Other through types as anonymous and distant from the Other as those employed by the indirect social observer of contemporaries. Both stand remote from the proximity of the we relationship where types are readily revisable and where, as Schutz says, one grows old together with the Other. This, of course, is not to deny that such scientific anonymity can permit clarification that might be difficult or impossible without the scientific *epoché*. Whatever privileged access the scientific observer possesses resembles the modes of access we have to each other in a reciprocal we relationship. In such a relationship, by having a different bodily perspective of the Other, I can become aware of much more than what the Other deliberately tries to communicate by my attending to his expressive movements. At the same time, though, my bodily perspective limits me, since I cannot know the complete historical past through which the Other has passed, the bodily tones he is feeling in the present, and so forth. In a similar fashion, the scientific *epoché* enhances the scientist's observational ability and the distribution of knowledge he can amass in regard to the Other, but the scientist's understanding of the Other is also vulnerable to the errors that anonymity and distance from the we relationship make inevitable.

These limits to the understanding of the Other, stemming from Schutz's philosophical description of the life world, not only indicate the boundaries for Weberian objectivity, they also specify the parameters for any attainment of objectivity by observing postulates that Schutz proposed in response to Nagel's demand for verifiability. Recall that Schutz, in order to ensure accurate compliance with the postulate of subjective interpretation, advances the postulate of adequacy, namely, that the typical construct of the scientist must be understandable for the actor himself.[34] In my judgment, however, the social scientist must finally decide when such understandability has been attained in his scientific attitude. It is according to his interpretation of the Other that he will have adequately understood the Other. Thus, however much the postulate of adequacy may provide a useful constraint for constructing scientific types, it does not facilitate an escape from the limits of *Verstehen* and scientific anonymity. Should the social scientist set aside the scientific attitude and converse with the life-world actor in order to evaluate his scientific type, his understanding of the life-world actor will still be restricted by limits of life-world *Verstehen;* that is, the social scientist can never understand the meanings of the Other exactly as the Other understands them, although he may be able to arrive at an understanding sufficient for his purposes.[35] Even seemingly complete agreement with the Other on what an expression or behavior means to him will conceal inevitable discrepancies in understanding, some possibly serious, that might only surface in later reflection.

In summary, *Phenomenology* provides social science with useful categories (*epoché, Verstehen,* typifications, because and in-order-to motives) and describes the general interpretive context in which social science is situated. In so doing, however, I maintain that *Phenomenology* unveils a limit to social-scientific objectivity beyond that surrounding any reflective endeavor. For however much the social scientist may make clear to the life-world actor what that actor himself never recognized, however much he may see about him what he does not see himself, however much predictability he may gain with reference to the behavior of the Other, and however much he may even come to agreement with the Other that he has adequately understood the Other, there is always a horizon of otherness known only to the Other that the social scientist can never supersede. The social scientist could only overstep this limit if he were the Other. The distribution of knowledge within one's consciousness and between people demarcates borders within which social science achieves its results.

5

The Distribution of Knowledge as Protophilosophy

Typifications as Essentially Social[1]

BESIDES PROVIDING a philosophical basis for the social sciences, Schutz's phenomenology also characterizes the life world toward which forms of phenomenology turn with their own unique reflective attitudes. A grasp of the life world, seen through the prism of the distribution of knowledge, casts not only our sociology but also our philosophy in a different hue. Schutz's account of the relationship between life-world type and philosophical eidos illustrates the significance of locating philosophical, eidetic reflection within the context of a prior philosophical anthropology. Before exploring the relationship between type and eidos, life world and eidetic phenomenology, we must examine briefly and more carefully the implications of Schutz's constitutive methodological approach to the life world for his theory of typification.

Schutz depends, of course, on Husserl's method of constitution, which is exemplified most clearly in Husserl's *Ideen II,* subtitled in German *Phänomenologische Untersuchungen zur Konstitution.* This text remained an unpublished manuscript during Husserl's lifetime, but during the fifteen years in which he labored over it, the question regarding the constitution of objects in consciousness had become the central problem of phenomenology for him, according to Marly Biemel, editor of the manuscript.[2] Schutz himself, in his commentary on Husserl's *Ideen II,* notes that Husserl personally informed him that he had left this second volume unpublished because he had not at that time found a satisfactory solution for the problem of intersubjectivity. Later, Husserl believed he had effectively dealt with that problem in his Fifth Cartesian Meditation.[3] Even if *Ideen II* did not adequately handle the problem of intersubjectivity in Husserl's opinion, it could still offer a valuable vantage point for understanding Husserl's theory of constitution.

Before Husserl attempts to constitute material nature in *Ideen II,* he explains how the theoretical attitude permits us to recover layers of meaning of which we are unaware in our lived experience of the object. This theoretical disclosure of the strata implicitly within a unity is nothing other than what Husserl means by constitution.[4]

Adopting this theoretical attitude, Husserl constitutes the material thing on which the natural sciences with their varying viewpoints focus. Husserl explores the essence of the material thing as distinct from animal realities whose psychological properties transcend the materiality in which they are founded and in which they secure a spatial definiteness. By the process of free variation, Husserl passes through a variety of real or imaginary material things in order to distill out those properties remaining invariant over all material objects. He concludes that in its essence, the material thing necessarily possesses a temporal span, a position within a spatial framework of relations, and spatial extension. Bodily extension, though, is not merely *a* property of material things; rather, it is *the* essential form of all real properties; extension is the grounding property, the essence fundament and form for all other determinations of the material thing. The material thing further consists in visual schemata (for example, it is necessarily colored) and tactual schemata (for example, solidity, elasticity, and flexibility in some degree characterize it).

These various properties necessary to the material thing are interrelated such that, for instance, color cannot appear without extension, and extension cannot appear without color.[5] Finally, it should be kept in mind that Husserl distinguishes between concrete sensory data, such as concrete colors, textures, shapes, and so forth, and color *simpliciter,* texture *simpliciter,* and shape *simpliciter.* These generic aspects of the material thing are gradually revealed in perceptual experience and reflectively ordered and interrelated in constitutive analysis.[6]

Interestingly enough, in such a constitutive procedure, withdrawing from the concrete to search for essential properties does not entail disregarding such concrete elements. Rather, invariant concrete elements are elevated to the status of essential properties, necessarily part of the eidos finally depicted. Concrete properties, such as colors, are taken into the constitution of the eidos material thing, which, of its essence, is colored in some way. As Husserl observed in his correspondence with Wilhelm Dilthey, the eidos embraces a multitude of concrete variations and relativities under its ideal laws and its configuration of essential properties.[7]

Husserl's constitution of the material thing in *Ideas II* warrants the following conclusions about the meaning of constitution itself:

1. The variation of concrete manifolds yields an essential unity with a set of essential properties.

2. The overarching unity (for example, the material thing) assumes preeminence over its essential properties, just as some properties (for example, extension) may take precedence over others (for example, coloredness).

3. These essential properties, however, stand in necessary relationships to each other and the overriding unity (for example, there can be neither a material thing that is not extended and colored nor extension and color that is apart from a material thing; nor can there be extension that is not colored and color that is not part of some extension).

4. Discovering essence does not involve flight from the lower levels that essence organizes, the strata *sedimented* within it,[8] but instead involves lifting invariant strata to the level of essential properties and grasping these strata in their essential, intrinsic relationship to that essence (for example, we do not ignore visual and tactual schemata in order to grasp the essence material thing but rather grasp their essential pertinence to that essence).

Schutz uses Husserl's constitutive methodology differently in accord with methodological strategies of *Phenomenology*. That is to say, he attempts a constitutive phenomenology of the natural attitude from within that natural attitude, accepting the social world as it is always accepted in everyday life or sociological investigation. Although for Husserl the constitution of material nature takes place within the solipsistic subject exercising phenomenological reduction, Schutz is not constrained by the limits of reduction and so includes the social that Husserl methodologically brackets. Schutz, in addition, does not survey a series of individual material objects in order to determine the essence of the material thing; rather, he is taking the entire natural attitude itself for his focus of examination. He varies the diverse social worlds in which human beings live their day-to-day lives in hopes of elucidating the unity and set of essential components of the social world. The invariant structures that Schutz unearths—the structure of consciousness, the corresponding forms of interpersonal understanding, and the spatiotemporal stratification of relationships—these invariant structures emerge from concrete social worlds and carry their sociality as one of their essential characteristics. In this, they resemble the material thing that emerges as invariant in contrast to its concrete exemplifications in their various colors, for instance, and yet coloredness (of some sort) will be an essential characteristic of the essence material thing.

Hence, typifications, that is, typified ways of conceiving the world and typified patterns of behavior, will vary from one social world or culture to another, but it is necessarily the case that if there is a sociocultural world, then its inhabitants will employ *some* set of typifications. It is also necessarily the case that those typifications will be social in nature, which, as Schutz points out, means that they are socially shared, transmitted, and reinforced, however different may be the concrete social ambiance in which they are embedded.[9] In brief, Schutz's application of constitutive methodology to the life world, and in particular to the typifications of the life world, yields a parallel with Husserl's constitution of the material thing, as Table 5.1 indicates. This table illustrates that social conditionedness is an essential property of typifications just as coloredness is essential to the material thing. In other words, sociality is one of the strands sedimented within the structure of life-world typifications, a strand that reflective analysis is always capable of disentangling and illuminating. Sociological reflection, recovering and revealing through empirical methods the influence of social groups on our typifications, parallels the investigative efforts of the theoretical attitude at work in phenomenological constitution on an essential plane.

The Social as Sedimented

Table 5.1

I Overarching Unities	II Material Thing	III Typification Structures
Essential properties accompanying the appearance of the unity and through which the unity appears	Extension, temporal span, location in a spatial framework, visual schemata (for example, coloredness), tactual schemata	Socially derived and reinforced, spatially and temporally located, used with reference to relevances
Concrete manifestations	Concrete appearances of concrete things with concrete properties	Concrete typifications in concrete social life worlds

It would be erroneous, given this table, to pit typification structures in general, derived as they are from the Husserlian theory of intentionality, against their concrete exemplifications in concrete *social* life worlds. General structures are not *invariant,* necessary, and *untouched by the social,* while concrete typifications are *variable,* contingent, and *socially derived.* Such a polarization, setting the invariant against the social, overlooks a basic insight flowing from Schutz's application of eidetic method to the natural attitude because it neglects the first entry of the third column. For Schutz, the social character of typifications is invariant and essential such that there cannot be typifications that do not reflect the social milieu from which they originate and in which they are used. The social is not just accidentally affixed to necessary structures of typifications whenever they are concretely instantiated, but it is intrinsically necessary to every life-world typification pattern.

This sedimentation of the social within typification structures leads to interesting conclusions paralleling those discussed in relation to Husserl's eidetic constitution of the material thing.

1. The variation of concrete typifying systems in concrete cultures yields the essential unity of a system of typifications with a set of essential properties, one of which is "being socially derived."

2. The overarching unity, typification system, takes precedence over its essential properties (for example, its social derivedness). Without constitutively analyzing this unity, it is possible to take for granted the social character of such typification systems or to consider their sociality an accidental result of their being instanced. Husserl's phenomenological reduction, which brackets the social, would be especially prone to such an omission unless it is complemented and undergirded by the Schutzian constitution of the life world toward which phenomenological reflection turns with its unique mode of attention.

3. The property of social derivedness is necessary to the overriding unity of a typification system in such a way that there cannot be a typification system that is not in some way socially derivative. Extending the analogy perhaps beyond legitimacy, we might venture to say that even to speak of social derivedness (social sharing, transmission, reinforcement) without a typification system carrying it is similar to speaking of coloredness apart from an extension. Typifications serve as a vehicle through which the social-group processes of sharing, transmission, and reinforcement take place with reference to the socialized individual.

4. Discovering the essence of typifications of the life world involves no flight from the social, but rather consists in both grasping the social as invariantly sedimented within such typifications and therefore upgrading the social to an essential property. As a result, typifications are intrinsically and essentially social in character.

This entire discussion of constitutive methodology and its implications for life-world typifications confirms and reiterates methodologically what Schutz's notion of the social distribution of knowledge already contains. The typifications through which we interpret our own experiences and each other in the life world are of necessity socially allocated. But what does this mean for higher level phenomenological, particularly eidetic reflection on the life world, especially since such eidetic reflection takes as its starting point the socially formed types of the life world?[9]

Type and Eidos, Sociality and Validity

In the concluding critical section of Schutz's essay, "Type and Eidos in Husserl's Late Philosophy," he suggests there is a mere difference of degree between type and eidos and that ideation can reveal nothing that was not preconstituted by the type.[10] Taking this comment as a clue, we can consider how eidetic reflection grows out of the natural attitude.

Empirical universals, which resemble eidetic universals in some aspects, illustrate clearly the continuity between life-world types and higher level universals. Both empirical and eidetic universals trace their origin back to the types through which individual objects are given to us in the life world.

> If we proceeded in our experiencing of this or that individual dog, we would find ever new characteristics which do not belong just to this individual dog, but to dogs in general, characteristics which are pre-delineated by the properties appropriated by us as typical for dogs in accordance with the incomplete and fugitive experiences we had had of them until now. This is the origin of a *presumptive idea of a universal* which surpasses the *concept* of *real* dogs as it originated in *real* experiences. Husserl calls this idea a presumptive one because we live continually in the empirical certainty—a certainty good until further notice—that what proves to be on the ground of known properties of an object of a particular type will also have all the further characteristics regularly discovered in other objects of this type by regular induction, and so on. In this manner the empirical concepts undergo continual change caused by the resorption of new characteristics under the guidance of the empirical idea of an open and always rectifiable concept, an idea which is at the foundation of our empirical faith in the continuity of our real experiences.[11]

These empirical universals are then elaborated by a method of comparison.

> Yet there are important differences between empirical universals and eidetic ones. The former are not only contingent in the sense that their formation starts from a particular given contingently in factual experience, but also in the sense that the conceptualization proceeds on the ground of comparison with likewise contingently given similarities.[12]

Such procedure yields a unique result: "Empirical concepts are not genuine specifications of pure universals; they mean typical generalizations, scopes of anticipations of experiences delineated by actual experiences."[13]

Eidetic universalization, in contrast, seizes on an experienced or phantasied objectivity as an example of the universal and a prototype for modifications by a series of free variations in phantasy in a procedure that is distinct from the method of induction.

> In the phenomenologically reduced sphere the phenomenon cube—the cube as it appears to me—keeps the same qualities as an intentional object of my perceiving act. But suppose I am interested in finding what are the qualities common to all cubes. I do not want to do so by the method of induction, which not only presupposes the existence of similar objects but also implies certain unwarranted logical assumptions. I have before me only this single concrete object perceived. I am free, however, to transform this perceived object in my fancy, by successively varying its features—its color, its size, the material of which it is made, its perspective, its illumination, its surrounding and background and so on. Thus I may imagine an infinite number of varied cubes. But these variations do not touch on a set of characteristics common to all imaginable cubes, such as rectangularity, limitation to six squares, corporeality. This set of characteristics, unchanged among all the imagined transformations of the concrete thing perceived—the kernel, so to speak, of all possibly imaginable cubes—I shall call the essential characteristics of the cube, or using a Greek term, the *eidos* of the cube. No cube can be thought of that would not have these essential features.[14]

Thus, the eidetic method aims at a different result from that intended by empirical universalization: namely, the invariant content, the inner structure, without which the object could not be the kind of object it is.

> All of these variations have concrete similarities with the same prototype, and the manifold of new images produced in phantasy is permeated by an invariant identical content in terms of which all the arbitrarily performed variations come to congruence, whereas their differences remain irrelevant. This invariant element prescribes the limits to all possible variations of the same prototype; it is that element without which an objectivity of this kind can neither be thought nor intuitively phantasied.[15]

> That which can be varied in arbitrary phantasying has necessarily an inner structure, an eidos, and therewith laws of necessity which determine the characteristics an objectivity must have in order to be of this or that particular kind.[16]

Eidetic universalization, beginning from what is given typically in life-world experience as a prototype, seeks to discover the necessary structure of what is thus given typically, the conditions of the possibility of there being such a given. Thus, unlike empirical generalizations, it does not take that typically given object for granted as anticipating a set of future experiences more or less clearly, depending on the degree of its elaboration by disciplined inductive experimentation. Hence, although there is *merely* a difference of degree between type and eidos, there is, nevertheless, a *difference* between them.

Husserl contrasts very clearly the contingent results produced by empirical universalization with the necessity yielded by eidetic universalization.

> Following experience's own train of sense, we can do nothing but project the indeterminate future world in the universal style of the past.
> But in this respect one consideration is striking: however much the expectations which are connected with actual and hypothetically assumed facts (in the latter case, hypothetically limited expectations) may guide us, we feel here[17] something of a strict necessity, such as we do not find in concrete empirical procedure and its expectations. Empirically we expect that the dog will snap at the bone tossed to him. But it does not *have* to be; it is no strict necessity. However, that the world can never be non-spatial, that everything is restricted to its generic structures—this seems necessary to us. Every felt necessity is an indicative sign of an a priori in the sense of an unconditioned, so called apodictic universality, which can be seen as such. Showing it is the test whether the felt necessity is a genuinely apodictic one, and not a confusion with a merely empirical indication.[18]

Schutz himself situates these eidetic procedures in relation to the life world, the focal point of his proto-philosophical-sociological analysis.

> The question of first importance which presents itself is whether the "free variations" to be performed in phantasy, starting from the individual object as example or prototype, are indeed as free as they seem, that is, whether the arbitrariness of transforming the empirically given into a special case of general possibilities does not have well-defined limits. To be sure, Husserl himself recognizes such limits when he speaks of regional ontologies or, in a terminology used by him in earlier writings, of spheres of incompatibility (*Unverträglich-keitssphären*). The freedom of variations in phantasy will not permit us to arrive, starting from the prototype of a colored object, at the eidos of sound. It is doubtless possible to grasp eidetically material realms or regions of being, but these regions are not constituted by performances of our consciousness: they are indeed ontological re-

gions of the world and, as such, given to our experience or, as we may say, imposed upon us.[19]

At this point, Schutz begins to ask a series of questions that seems to envision the life-world experience itself as setting the bounds within which eidetic reflection operates.

> But we have to drive the questioning even further. Is it possible, by means of free variations in phantasy, to grasp the eidos of a concrete species or genus, unless these variations are limited by the frame of the type in terms of which we have experienced, in the natural attitude, the object from which the process of ideation starts as a familiar one, as such and such an object within the life-world? Can these free variations in phantasy reveal anything else but the limits established by such typification? If these questions have to be answered in the negative, then there is indeed merely a difference of degree between type and eidos. Ideation can reveal nothing that was not preconstituted by the type.[20]

Just as Schutz's protophilosophy and protosociology trace the more embracive context within which we exercise phenomenological reduction, so also eidetic analysis, whether it follows on reduction or not, presupposes what the protophilosophy and protosociology describe. Thus the social formation of concrete typifications through which experience is given, which underlies phenomenological reduction but to which reduction's particular attitudinal focus does not permit it to attend, also undergirds the constitution of the eidos. This is so however much eidetic analysis, because of its frequent reliance on reduction and its preoccupation with its own internal procedures, may remain oblivious to its own life-world foundation.

In my opinion, the connection between type and eidos, on the one hand, and the distinctiveness of eidetic methodology and its results, on the other, reveal a circular relationship. Socially conditioned types ground eidetic analyses, and eidetic analyses specify the conditions necessary for the types that ground them.

As we move from type to eidos, the types of the life world circumscribe and condition the conclusions of eidetic investigation.[21] The prototype that forms the basis for free variations is itself given through life worldly, that is, socially conditioned, typifications. Hence, to take Schutz's own example, would it be possible to undertake an eidetic analysis of a cube if a prior sociolinguistic system did not exist by which we are able to pick out a cube from its background horizon? Further, do not the imaginative variations through which the philosopher passes in an effort to disclose the eidos depend on socially derived norms governing type usage in the life world and prescribing those bounds within which an object may be legitimately altered? It is even tempting to speculate that the rule of synthesis to which the eidetic universal refers may itself be molded under the constant inducement of those same socially established norms to which the philosopher may not be consciously attending. Finally, at the end of eidetic analysis, the result cannot exceed the bounds that such life-world, socially conditioned typifications set for us. Hence, Schutz's effort to depict the relationship between eidetic methodology and the life world makes possible, perhaps as never before, an awareness of the social mechanisms on which eidetic analysis relies. The sociality of the life world makes possible the discovery of the eidos.[22]

Nevertheless, can we reduce the meaning of the eidos to the social conditions of its discovery, since eidos differs from type? Eidetic analysis involves a greater degree of reflective disengagement from lived immersion in typifications and norm-directed behavior than empirical universalization. Empirical universalization proceeds presumptively (until counter evidence surfaces) and moves inductively from one similar object to another, taking for granted the social typifications by which one object is identified prereflexively as similar to another. Eidetic analysis, on the contrary, does not even permit the movement to another similar object without first stopping to analyze the characteristics constitutive of the single object perceived. In so doing, eidetic analysis attempts to clarify the essential properties that the socially formed typifications, through which concrete object are given, naïvely presuppose. But still, it might be objected that, in spite of this reflective disengagement, a kind of eidetic *epoché*, our lived experience remains active, unconsciously prompting the choices we make in articulating eidetic conclusions.

Even if that were true, the eidos itself seems to contain something more than the prototypes and norms that lead to its discovery and the life-world typifications with which it is compared afterward. In fact, that something more consists in the clear unveiling of the definitional properties without which life worldly prototypes, imaginative variations, and verificatory typifications could not be what they are. Similarly, the rule of synthesis uncovered by eidetic procedure underlies the social norms governing type usage that guide, coax, and prompt the philosopher, even without his advertence, in his search for this rule of synthesis. For these norms presuppose a set of essential properties pertinent to the type whose usage they regulate. The protoypes, variations, norms, and typifications thus implicitly take for granted what eidetic scrutiny articulates and measure themselves against it, as Schutz suggests: "Thus we obtain the eidos as the intuited or intuitable pure universal which, not conditioned by any fact, precedes all conceptualizations in the sense of 'meanings of words'; on the contrary, all pure concepts have to be formed as adjusted to the eidos."[23]

The socially determined typifications and guiding norms serve as stages, as it were, leading to the discovery of the eidos that stipulates the very traits necessary and preconditional for the very identity of those typifications and norms.

It is possible, then, to approach eidetic claims either in relationship to their life worldly social determinants or in regard to their a priori essentialism. Schutz's theory of motivation correlates with this duality of perspectives, while also helping preserve their distinctiveness and irreducibility. First of all, someone engaged in an eidetic project has adopted the in-order-to motive of attempting to spell out the essential characteristics presupposed by some lived typification. For the most part, while engaged in this project, he is unaware of the because motives, the social and environmental determinants, affecting his project.

> On the contrary, there is no evidence to support the view that the actor ever has any awareness of the because-motive of his action. This applies to one who is establishing a meaning as well as to any other actor. To be sure, he lives through the subjective experiences and intentional Acts which I have interpreted as his because-motive.[24]

It is only after completing the in-order-to project (here eidetic articulation) that he can seek out its because motives.

> Now, we have already seen that we can go beyond the in-order-to motive and seek out the because-motive. Of course, knowledge of the latter presupposes in every case knowledge of the former. The subjective meaning-context which is the in-order-to motive must first be seen and taken for granted as an already constituted object in itself before any venture into deeper levels is undertaken.[25]

As Schutz notes in another place, investigation into the because motives presupposes that the motivated experience is over and involves the discovery of determinants of that experience in pluperfect tense.

> The formulation of a genuine why-question is generally possible only after the motivated experience has occurred and when one looks back on it as something whole and complete in itself. The motivating experience in turn is past once again in relation to the motivated one, and we can therefore designate our intentional reference to it as *thinking in the pluperfect tense* . . . The meaning-context of the true because-motive is thus always an explanation after the event.[26]

In the intersubjective, interactive, dialogic situation of philosophical discourse,[27] the person developing and articulating an eidetic claim anticipates that his eidetic statements will function as a because motive for his philosophizing partner. In the same way, a questioner expects his question to become the because motive of his answerer's reply. Usually, the respondent is so immediately taken up with his response, with the *project* of responding, his own in-order-to project, that he can only subsequently, in retrospect, become aware that the prior statement of his cophilosopher served as the because motive eliciting and framing his own project of response. Just as the question constitutes the framework within which the questioner anticipates a response and the respondent usually answers, so also in philosophical dialogue, an author intends his eidetic claim to evoke either agreement or disagreement on the part of his dialogue partner in regard to his attribution of necessary characteristics to an eidos. Should the respondent to an eidetic claim begin a lengthy discussion of the social background of that claim's author and thereby explain how the claim came about, he would, in most cases, have undertaken a project of response totally unanticipated by that claim's author.

Thus, it seems, an eidetic claim, indeed any kind of validity claim, once completed, can stimulate two very diverse responses on the part of a dialogue partner. On the one hand, the claim can act as a because motive of an in-order-to project whose goal is to explain why the claim is valid or why it is not. Such a project would involve no consideration of the pluperfect events motivating the author to make or form the claim as he did. On the other hand, we can start with the completed validity claim and embark on the project of discovering those pluperfect, social, environmental conditions that formed the because motives of the author's claim. This latter project would probably circumvent the author's expectations of how his claim was going to be received.[28]

Parallelisms between both types of investigations, namely, that in each, a completed in-order-to project of an author functions as the because motive of the in-order-to project of a respondent, has perhaps concealed their fundamental difference. The in-order-to project aimed at responding to a validity claim on its own terms (which does not preclude disputing the validity criteria involved) is far different from an in-order-to project attempting to unearth the because motives of that same claim. The confusion of these two projects, which can both be adopted in relation to the *same* claim, may well account for the fact that some sociologists of knowledge have felt that their examinations could undermine the validity of claims. Of course, where irresolvable differences emerge between dialogue partners over the validity of a claim or its criterion of validity, we might well retreat to an inquiry into the because motives underlying such a division of opinion. But, then, we have significantly altered the entire investigative project from the question of validity establishment itself and directed it toward the social conditions of the validity criteria. The irreducibility and distinctiveness of the social conditioning and a priori essentialism of eidetic claims can be defined by carefully attending to both the in-order-to project of the author along with his dialogic expectations and to the different in-order-to motives governing the two divergent analytic projects possible in the face of that author's claim.

Finally, for Schutz the quest for because motives falls under the paradigm of hermeneutics rather than that of causation.

> And since every interpretation in the pluperfect tense is determined by the Here and Now from which it is made, the choice of *which* past experiences are to be regarded as the genuine because-motive of the project depends on the cone of light which the Ego lets fall on its experiences preceding the project.[29]

In conclusion, I would argue that Schutz's turn to the life world in his protophilosophy and protosociology brings into focus those life-world social processes in relation to which eidetic procedure is carried on, since there is merely a difference of *degree* between type and eidos. The influence of the social distribution of knowledge reaches even into the loftiest of eidetic speculations. At the same time, however, there is a *difference,* and eidetic analysis distinctively concentrates on disclosing the conditions of the possibility of the types and underlying typified courses of action leading to eidetic discovery. Furthermore, eidetic claims lend themselves to two divergent projects of response, specifically, that of confirming or disconfirming the validity of those claims or that of going behind them to bring to light their pluperfect determinants. The clear demarcation of these two autonomous but compatible spheres of investigation permits the achievement of Schutz's dream, that is, it gives large scope to the impact of the social without abandoning the core of Husserl's eidetic methodology.

The essay "Type and Eidos," showing the relation between eidos and life world, depends on the eidetic presentation of the life world in *Phenomenology.* At the same time, the eidetically wrought *Phenomenology* relies on the method of eidetic investigation outlined within that later essay. This mutual implication would be self-undermining if the social origins of *Phenomenology,* suggested by "Type and Eidos," would disqualify its essential truth. Since, as we have just argued, that need not be the case, the interrelationship of these two works of Schutz indicates rather that Schutz has achieved his goal, namely, to fuse Husserlian epistemological analysis with the sociality of the life world in the creation of a new epistemology of the social world.

6

The Distribution of Knowledge and the Sociology of Knowledge

WHAT BEARING does Schutz's account of the life world, where knowledge is distributed by space, time, and social affiliation, have on the sociology of knowledge? Schutz's phenomenology, in the first place, can unravel the paradox of the sociology of knowledge as Ernst Grünwald presents it. Secondly, Schutz's work provides a setting within which the traditional sociology of knowledge, originating from and following the lead of Marx, can find its proper location. Finally, this situating of the traditional sociology of knowledge in reference to Schutz's description of the life world exhibits intersubjective processes and limits that the sociology of knowledge has tended to disregard.

The Paradox of the Sociology of Knowledge: Reconciling the Social and the Valid, Essential Analysis and Relativism[1]

Three methodological strategies define *Phenomenology:* the inclusion of the social world, a focus on meaning structures, and eidetic analysis. Schutz's implementation of this methodology results in a description of life-world typifications as invariantly social.[2] On the basis of Schutz's methodology and the typification structures it illuminates, we can dissolve the paradox of the sociology of knowledge while also expanding on one of its essential premises.

Grünwald provides us with a rendition of the paradox. It is sociological relativism, engendered by the sociology of knowledge's recognition of the role of social conditioning, which leads to the paradox, in Grünwald's opinion.

> There is no need for an extensive investigation to make it clear that this variety of sociologism is a form of scepticism and therewith eliminates itself as contradictory. For the claim that all thinking is socially bound and therefore can make no claim to truth itself makes a claim to truth.[3]

Analyzing Grünwald's argument, we might say that the sociological relativist, prompted by the findings of sociology of knowledge, begins by affirming

1. If *x* is a claim to truth, then *x* is socially conditioned.

However, he goes on to add

2. If *x* is socially conditioned, then *x* cannot claim to be true.

But then the antirelativist, such as Grünwald, can convert statements 1 and 2 into logical premises that lead to the logical conclusion (statement 5):

3. Statement 1 is a claim to truth (by definition).

4. Statement 1 is socially conditioned (*modus ponens*, statements 3, 1).

5. Statement 1 cannot claim to be true (by *modus ponens*, statement 4, 2).

Thus, the social relativist's argument turns back on the very premise that the sociology of knowledge bequeathed to him as a starting point.

The Schutzian perspective can disentangle this paradox by confuting statement 2. For *Phenomenology*, it is impossible to have access to objects or people, formulate propositions about them, and so make and verify truth claims except through socially transmitted systems of typifications. The socially conditioned character of a truth claim not only does not obstruct the possibility of its truth, no truth can be achieved except through a socially conditioned perspective. Schutz, thus, would concur with Merleau-Ponty's insight that "whatever truth we may have is to be gotten not in spite of but through our historical inherence."[4]

But what do Schutz and Grünwald here mean by truth? Does truth signify for them discursively grounded propositions, as it does for Habermas? Of course, this definition, Habermas himself admits, presupposes identifiable objects to which predicates can be assigned. Or do Schutz and Grünwald agree with Husserl that truth involves a fulfilling synthesis of identification between the object as meant and the object as given? In either case, it seems, concepts of truth always build on an a prior stratum of objects that must, in the end, be given through typifications. It is not imperative that Schutz spell out his own notion of truth, since his efforts center rather on the primordial layer of meaning establishment on which later ideas of truth depend, whether these ideas be

Husserlian, Habermasian, or of some other type. As J. N. Mohanty has observed, the task of phenomenology involves scrutinizing the meanings presuppositional to the concept of truth. In so doing, Mohanty contends, the phenomenologist "is not providing a guarantee that a truth which one may happen to regard as being true in itself is really so."[5]

It is conceivable that Schutz, by reason of his methodology, which conjoins the typifications through which truth can be attained with sociality, would have found himself in agreement with the recently developed Strong Programme for the Sociology of Science. That program has attempted to break down the artificial opposition between the logical and natural (the true), on the one hand, and the cultural and social, on the other.[6] Such an opposition may have originated because certain modes of thought pretended to have achieved truth apart from a sociohistorical context. Sociological relativism, however, by sacrificing the possibility of truth on the altar of social determinism, merely inverts this same discordance between truth and social conditioning without overcoming it. Only a viewpoint such as Schutz's, which understands social conditioning and truth claiming as inseparably intertwined, can undo this basic supposition of sociological relativism. Once the relativist's second premise is disproved, the paradox of the sociology of knowledge to which it leads collapses.

Of course, our earlier extension of Schutz's theory of motivation to the dialogic setting of claiming eidetic truth, applies to any process of truth claiming.[7] Since we can respond to any truth claim by accepting or disputing its validity in accord with its author's in-order-to motives or by exploring the because motives effecting the claim, it is possible for claims to be both true and yet socially formed at the same time.

Social conditioning threatens the possibility of truth claims not only because those claims draw on a prior reserve of socially constituted meanings. In addition, the criteria of validity that claims must satisfy to be true are social creations, shared, passed on, and reinforced. But, due to Schutz's distinction between the kinds of motives, it is possible to argue whether a claim satisfies criteria or whether those criteria themselves are adequate without *at the same time* discussing the social milieu in which those criteria are embedded.[8] In spite of the separability of these questions, though, we need not deny the social situatedness of such validity criteria whose social genesis can be examined by a retrospectively directed because-motive investigation.

The Schutzian position, however, shows its sympathy for the relativist's point of view (and the sociology of knowledge from which it flows) by Schutz's delineation of the important role of because motives and by his methodological fusion of the social with the intentional. Although the synthesis of these latter two elements has assumed prominence in criticism of the second proposition of the relativist, the eidetic quality of Schutz's depiction of the life world comes to the fore with regard to the first assertion. The eidetic dimension of *Phenomenology* actually lends support to that assertion by unfolding fully what underlies the relativist's tenet that all claims to truth are socially conditioned. This eidetic thread in Schutz's phenomenology leads to insistence on certain *necessary* truths about the life world that, as *necessary* truths, most sociological relativists would be reluctant to admit. For Schutz, it is necessarily the case that we interpret the world through concrete typifications that are necessarily socially derived. In my opinion, then, Schutz's phenomenology leads to the conclusion that relativism is essential.

In fact, whenever someone raises relativistic claims, he does so on some essential basis that often remains unthematized. Thus, he who would allege relativism because all truth is incarnated in a situation, for instance, as Merleau-Ponty has demonstrated, or he who, following Sartre, would espouse relativism because an appeal to objective essences is only bad faith covering up one's own exercise of freedom—these standpoints both presuppose certain views of how the life world is structured (that is, in regard to the nature of perception or human freedom), however much their advocates may refrain from making explicit such presuppositions. And, of course, to admit such presuppositions would require a further effort to clarify and develop them, as Merleau-Ponty and Sartre have done. Husserl's own assault on scepticism in "Philosophy As Rigorous Science" involved a similar scepticism about scepticism itself, since its own evasive, asserting-without-asserting, reflective style inevitably conceals assumptions in need of positive attention.[9]

Perhaps, however, the relativistic critic might dispute Schutz's claim to have spelled out the universal, a priori eidos of the social world on the grounds that no one can escape those social, spatial, and historical determinants conditioning all knowledge—not even Schutz. Such a criticism, on the one hand, draws its strength from the mistaken supposition underlying the second relativist assertion, namely, that sociohistorical conditioning prohibits a claim to truth. On the other hand, this critic also firmly believes in the first premise of relativism, the essential claim, namely, that all claims to truth are socially conditioned. After all, he is in fact arguing that it is necessarily and essentially the case that no one can escape social, historical, and spatial determinants in fashioning truth claims. We cannot unloose the paradoxical character of this relativist position by only healing the rift between the true and the social in the second relativist tenet. Some reflection is also needed on the paradoxical character of the first tenet of relativism, which is an essential declaration of relativism.

But in pointing to the historical, social, and spatial limitations of

Schutz's phenomenology, is the relativist not presupposing Schutz's eidos of the life world in criticizing it but in a vaguer, less articulate form than that in which Schutz has presented it? The first premise of relativism, that all claims to truth are socially conditioned, resembles *Phenomenology*, which, I would argue, also essentially affirms the truth of relativism. Schutz's phenomenology expands and develops what is latent within the condensed first premise of sociological relativism.

But why does the sociological relativist prefer to criticize the Schutzian eidos of the life world even though it expounds in detail the relativist's own convictions? Why does the social relativist play the sceptic in regard to others' eidetic affirmations without positively accounting for his own critical perspective? Why this evasive style unless the relativist believes that relativism and eidetic assertion are unavoidably at odds with each other? Here, another operative, but often unexamined assumption, paralleling the early supposition that social conditioning obstructs truth claims, emerges: Eidetic analysis and relativism are antipathetic. Schutz's work, then, can be seen to display the harmony possible between these supposed antagonists by outlining the eidetic structures of which every form of relativism implicity makes use. In so doing, Schutz merely confirms what the sociology of knowledge finds and at the same time overleaps its paradoxical pitfalls.

Marx and the Schutzian Architectonic

The philosophical roots of the sociology of knowledge trace themselves back to Plato's cave and Bacon's idols. During the Enlightenment, extensive criticism focused on the socially induced prejudices and distortions in the psychology of the human knower that block access to truth. Karl Marx shared the Enlightenment's mistrust of the immediate contents of consciousness. For instance, following Feuerbach, Marx attacks religion for involving false projections of the human self into the "fantastic reality of heaven," which prevent us from facing up to true human reality.[10]

Although Enlightenment sceptics would have agreed with Marx for stripping away the socially engendered illusions of religion, according to Marx the criticism of religion was but the premise of criticism. It was an unmasking of self-alienation in its sacred form that was to lead to unmasking self-alienation in its secular form, a critique that should have passed into criticism of law and politics. In Marx's view, the Young Hegelians, who set about criticizing philosophy and religion, never left those realms. Their criticism remained within the framework of philosophy and religion and did not extend to the political, legal, social, and, especially, economic realms. In spite of their "world-shaking" statements, these radicals were actually conservatives, since they did not address underlying economic and social realities.[11]

As Marx points out, criticism of material economic conditions of production takes priority over the criticism of ideas:

> With the change of the economic foundation the entire immense superstructure is more or less rapidly transformed. In considering such transformations a distinction should always be made between the material transformation of the economic conditions of production, which can be determined with the precision of natural science, and the legal, political, religious, aesthetic or philosophic—in short, ideological forms in which men become conscious of this conflict and fight it out. Just as our opinion of an individual is not based on what he thinks of himself, so can we not judge such a period of transformation by its own consciousness; on the contrary, this consciousness must be explained rather from the contradictions of material life, from the existing conflict between the social productive forces and the relations of production.[12]

Hence, Marx urges us to take his analytic starting point not from consciousness, but from those material, economic conditions that determine consciousness.

> In direct contrast to German philosophy, which descends from heaven to earth, here one ascends from earth to heaven. In other words, to arrive at man in the flesh, one does not set out from what men say, imagine, or conceive, nor from man as he is described, thought about, imagined, or conceived. Rather one sets out from real active men and their actual life-process and demonstrates the development of ideological reflexes and echoes of that process. The phantoms formed in the human brain, too, are necessary sublimations of man's material life process which is empirically verifiable and connected with material premises. Morality, religion, metaphysics, and all the rest of ideology and their corresponding forms of consciousness no longer seem to be independent. They have no history or development. Rather, men who develop their material production and their material relationships alter their thinking and the products of their thinking along with their real existence. Consciousness does not determine life, but life determines consciousness. In the first view the starting point is consciousness taken as a living individual; in the second it is the real living individuals themselves as they exist in real life, and consciousness is considered only as *their* consciousness.[13]

Marx's discovery that ideas depend on material factors led him to oppose the tradition that had regarded those ideas as independent of material factors and to shift his emphasis to an analysis of just those material factors.[14] After Marx, as Grünwald has shown, Marxist sociology has tended to regard the subjective meanings of the individual as irrelevant. It has adopted an antipsychological stance in order to avoid bourgeois sociology's preoccupation with the social actor's psychical acts and its resultant neglect of the true problems of social and economic being, even as Marx opposed the Young Hegelians.[15]

Finally, Marx's inquiry into ideology relies on Hegel. For Hegel, all history manifests the absolute spirit, which in its cunning is able to use for its own purposes human agents so preoccupied with their own mundane interests that they are unaware of being the tools and organs of the spirit. So also for Marx, morality, religion, metaphysics, and the rest of ideology manifest economic relationships behind the backs of the ideologists themselves.[16]

Marx's suspicion about the immediate contents of human consciousness and his consequent turn to the macro-level manifestation relationship between the economic substructure and the cultural superstructure have framed the context in which most later sociology of knowledge has been discussed. Major questions have surfaced about the relationship between the substructure and the superstructure (with Robert Merton listing at least twenty-six different possibilities);[17] whether they are mutually determinative and in what degree;[18] how these two elements are themselves to be defined;[19] and whether to begin the sociology of knowledge with the superstructure or the substructure.[20] Associated with these problems, which presuppose Marx's manner of posing the question, is the matter of predictability, namely, whether certain cultural phenonmena or individual meaning structures can be predicted from the particular social relationships to which they belong.[21] Moreover, whenever *Wissenssoziologie* attempts to make predictions from a substructural base, it inevitably turns up anomalous patterns, such as proletarians who do not have proletarian consciousness for Marx or middle-class existentialists who do not accept universalistic achievement norms for Parsons. According to some sociologists, these anomalous patterns place in question the basic principles of the traditional sociology of knowledge deriving from Marx and call for a discipline based on other premises.[22] Finally, the lack of predictability in such cases raises the question of whether the sociology of knowledge can be scientific.[23] The preceding questions are connected, too, with the problem of reductionism; that is, whether the superstructure can be explained without residue by the substructure; whether economics is the sole determinant or the most forceful; whether there is an interplay between several substructural determinants; and whether the superstructure can react back on the substructure.[24]

Not only have the *problems* of sociology of knowledge generally been posed in accord with the model of a manifestation relationship between substructure and superstructure, but virtually all the major *figures* in the sociology of knowledge have discussed the problems in these terms. A cursory glance at such thinkers as Marx, Scheler,[25] Weber,[26] Mannheim,[27] Merton,[28] and Parsons[29] will bear out this claim.

Schutz's thought presents us with an overall philosophical architectonic within which this traditional sociology of knowledge that took its cue from Marx can be placed. This architectonic consists of three levels. At the first level would be Schutz's protosociology and protophilosophy, his *Phenomenology*, an eidetic description of the socialized typification patterns of the life world to which phenomenological reflection (for example, reduction, eidetic analysis) turns as well as the various kinds of sociological analyses that can be situated at higher levels in the architectonic. The second level would include analyses of concrete meaning structures in interpersonal relationships, examples of which are to be found in the *verstehenden* sociology and Schutz's own constructed types of the stranger or the homecomer, all of which might use categories developed by Schutz at level one. Such types are "constructs of the constructs formed in common-sense thinking by actors on the social scene."[30] Finally, at the third level, the social scientist abstracts from these particular concrete encounters between human beings to form generalizations, laws, and institutional and functional analyses. Marxian efforts to correlate cultural achievements with their substructural roots belong here also. Schutz remarks:

> It is true that a very great part of the social sciences can be performed and has been performed at a level which legitimately abstracts from all that happens in the individual actor. But this operating with generalizations and idealizations on a high level of abstraction is in any case nothing but a kind of intellectual shorthand. Whenever the problem under inquiry makes it necessary, the social scientist must have the possibility of shifting the level of his research to that of individual human activity, and where the real scientific work is done this shift will always become possible.[31]

Schutz believes that his own system can accommodate abstract, higher level economic laws, such as the law of formation of rates of exchange, the law of profit, the law of population, and other such propositions, laws that do not refer to any individual or spatiotemporal collection of individuals.[32] He adds, though, the proviso that it must always be possible for us to return to the forgotten man of the social sciences, the actor in the social world whose doing and feeling lie at the basis of the whole social system and whose behavior is taken account of at the lower two levels of Schutz's overarching architectonic. It is at the upper third level that most research in the sociology of knowledge has been carried on since Marx gave the sociology of knowledge its initial direction.

Interestingly enough, this differentiation of levels progressively aban-
dons the three basic methodological components of the first level,
Schutz's *Phenomenology.* While Schutz's phenomenology involves (1) an
essential description of (2) meaning structures that in their empirical
manifestations result from (3) social processes and structure, the *verstehende* sociology drops the essential analysis to examine concrete, socially established meaning structures. The third-level investigations
generally prescind from meaning analyses to focus on concrete social
processes and structures.

Furthermore, these levels mutually complement each other. The first
level offers a philosophical foundation for the second by furnishing it
with a set of descriptive categories. The third level abstracts from the
first two levels but yields results that can be retranslated into terms of
those lower levels. Likewise, through the correlations and laws of the
third level, we can better understand those institutional patterns or
behavioral frequencies and regularities in accordance with, or contrary
to, which individuals in any interpersonal encounter described at level
two are acting. Indeed, research at level three can also serve to disclose
the latent functions or false consciousness of those meaning structures
portrayed in level-two endeavors.[33]

In the context of this architectonic, Schutz's Husserlian origins and his
egological starting point become apparent, since his work, while lending
itself readily to tasks of the *verstehenden* sociology, stands at the opposite
pole from studies concentrating on the study of institutions and social
structures. Still, Schutz's theory presents us with a thoroughly socialized
view of the individual that is already aimed toward, and of a piece with,
those higher-level structural analyses of whose importance Schutz was
completely convinced. We cannot argue fairly that Schutz thought his
own foundational work or the *verstehende* sociology with which it is so
compatible constituted the whole of sociology, the most valuable sociology, or the prescriptive pattern for all successful sociology. Sociology
of knowledge as launched by Marx has a legitimate place at the third
level within the Schutzian architectonic.[34]

The Foundation, Extent, and Limits of the Sociology of Knowledge: The Elusive Other

Several beneficial results ensue from placing the traditional sociology
of knowledge within the Schutzian architectonic. In the first place,
Phenomenology secures an epistemological base for the sociology of
knowledge. Schutz's depiction of the socialized typification patterns presents the object of the sociology of knowledge, the life word with its
divergent knowledge distributions, in a way coherent with that discipline

itself. Schutz's phenomenology also permits the sociology of knowledge to escape its own paradox by revealing the compatibility between sociality and truth claims and essential assumptions and relativism.

Secondly, Schutz's findings supplement the abstractive character of the sociology of knowledge. The traditional sociology of knowledge, because of its preoccupation with third-level correlations between the substructure and the superstructure, has tended to neglect the subjective meanings of individual actors, the forgotten men from whom it abstracts. Functionalist sociology, according to sociologist George Homans, has likewise focused on the functions and dysfunctions of social systems, all the while covertly presupposing psychological propositions about the needs, motives, skills, and values of individual men, whether functional theorists admit this or not.[35] Homans traces this evasion of psychological explanations, what might be called a "flight from meaning," to Durkheim's effort to preserve the independence of sociology in contrast to psychology.[36] Was not Marx, the initiator of sociology of knowledge, impelled toward a similar flight from meaning by his suspicion of meanings emerging from production relations on which he preferred to concentrate? But if sociologists of knowledge wish to shift their attention to individual activity, as should always be possible according to Schutz, *Phenomenology* stands ready at hand. Using its honed categories for describing thought and action (for example, typifications, relevances, because and in-order-to motives, we and they relationships), the sociology of knowledge can descend from abstraction with Husserlian rigor.

Unfortunately, because of the sociology of knowledge's abstractive level and flight from meaning, it has veered from the course on which Weber had set sociology as a separate science because it interprets not inert objects but beings who themselves interpret their worlds. But even where the sociology of knowledge has taken account of intersubjective understanding, it has often surmised too soon that it has understood the meaning of the Other, particularly in its zeal to show that meaning's social bondedness. But if the distribution of knowledge has brought to light anything, it has shown how elusive the subjective meaning of the Other is. There is a necessary and permanent incommensurability between the meaning intended by one person and that interpreted by the Other. This incommensurability can become all the more conspicuous as our types are more abstract and anonymous, as are the sociologist's. The sociologist will be even more prone to misunderstand if he regards the meaning of the Other as an irrelevant epiphenomenon to be quickly demythologized and dispensed with. The Schutzian phenomenological base performs a third service for the sociology of knowledge by reminding it of the domain of intersubjective understanding whose intricacies it cannot afford to overlook. Thus, the Schutzian architectonic holds Marx and Weber in tension; each needs the other.[37]

These difficulties in interpreting concrete human actors, from which the normal sociology of knowledge may have kept clear by abstractly concentrating on substructural and superstructural correlations, have always reasserted themselves in anomalous patterns of behavior. Such patterns have upset efforts at prediction and reduction at times to the detriment of sociology of knowledge's basic principles and even its scientific character.[38]

Schutz's theory of consciousness and the distribution of knowledge make a fourth contribution to traditional sociology of knowledge by explaining, at the level of essence, *why* there are problems of predictability in the social sciences and why anomalies occur. For Schutz, each human being is unique in that he passes through his own history of experiences in his own particular order, encountering events, people, and social groups in varying intensities. Each new experience alters the accumulated stock of knowledge at hand, including the protentions and expectations of future events, people, and institutions. The effect that any event, person, or institution will have on someone will depend on how he interprets what is given to him, and how he interprets depends on his whole history up to that moment. Therefore, to be able to predict what the Other will do in any given situation in reaction to group or institutional pressures presupposes we have passed through all the Other's experiences in their order and intensity. But then, as Schutz observes, we would have to be the Other. For Schutz, as for Bergson, the density of *durée* determines the limits of predictability.[39]

Furthermore, the Schutzian notion of consciousness resists reductionistic comprehension because the pattern of someone's membership in *several* past and present groups makes it unlikely that he would respond with rigid consistency to any *single* group's influence. In addition, the interlocking factors distributing knowledge, that is, time, space, and social affiliation, arise in a consciousness whose complexity withstands simplification. Any reductionistic sociology of knowledge, which would abstract from this web of factors to narrow in on how our participation in an economic group alone determines our knowledge configuration, will inevitably arrive at one-sided conclusions.

The anomalies of unpredictability and irreducibility on which the traditional sociology of knowledge often runs aground bring to the surface once again what we earlier described as the second limit to social-scientific objectivity: the otherness of the Other.[40] The otherness of the Other also circumscribes the sociology of knowledge. However much predictability the sociologist may gain in regard to the Other or however profound his grasp of the Other's socioeconomic determinants, of which the Other himself may be heedless, the Other can never be known as he knows himself. There remains an essential disproportionality between meanings intended by one person and meanings interpreted by another due to the essentially different ways their distributions of knowledge have been built up. Schutz's phenomenology, which fuses Weber's concern for subjective meaning with Husserlian internal time consciousness, fulfills a fifth function for the standard sociology of knowledge by never allowing it to forget the necessary incompleteness of our knowledge of the Other.

In highlighting the otherness of the Other, Schutz's phenomenology takes far more seriously than any reductionistic sociology of knowledge the extent and complexity of the impact of the social on us. A reductionistic sociology of knowledge might construe an individual's distribution of knowledge as corresponding to only his participation in his present economic group. But why should other social affiliations and our history of affiliation be excluded? Although Schutz saw clearly, as did Durkheim, that the individual is a product of the *conscience collective*,[41] he went beyond Durkheim in concurring with Simmel that a unique confluence of diverse past and present social streams forms the current that is each unique individual.[42]

As a result, Schutz's discovery of the otherness of the Other unveils a social world that is also more thoroughly relativistic than the traditional sociology of knowledge usually recognizes. *Phenomenology* uncovers a social-individual relativism that, paradoxically, is essential and surfaces within the simplest of human encounters. The divisions between classes and social groups that the sociology of knowledge catalogs are extensions from the root dividedness and relativity of every human individual in relation to every other due to the spatial, historical, and socioeconomical factors from which each emerges. For this reason, Schutz argued that the so-called sociology of knowledge has approached the more embracive problem of the social distribution of knowledge merely from the angle of the ideological foundation of truth in its dependence on social and, especially, economic conditions.[43] There will always remain a relativity and residue of unknowability in the comprehension of the Other as long as the Other must be understood relative to the nuances of another's typification and relevance system, whether the Other be the bourgeois owner of a factory, a fellow proletarian, a marriage partner of fifty years, or even an identical twin.

Finally, Schutz's rational recovery of the limits of the knowable in a way reminiscient of Kantian critique also revives the authentic spirit of the sociology of knowledge. The original inspiration of sociology of knowledge in Marx aimed at breaking down smug forms of rationalism that could hermetically fend off whatever might question argument itself. Unfortunately, the sociology of knowledge has deteriorated at times into the very rationalism it came to combat. It has assumed that it could comprehend the Other, categorically circumscribe him, or even dismiss him by facilely bringing to light his social and, in particular, his economic alliances. Schutz's work, by placing at the foundation of the sociology of knowledge the never-to-be intellectually mastered otherness of the Other, challenges the sociologist's self-centered interpretations and invites him to acknowledge his discipline's own horizons and begin anew the infinite task of understanding the Other.

Notes

Because the following works appear so frequently, these abbreviations are used:

CP, 1 Alfred Schutz, *Collected Papers*, vol. 1, *The Problem of Social Reality*, edited and introduced by Maurice Natanson with preface by H. L. Van Breda (Hague: Martinus Nijhoff, 1962).

CP, 2 Alfred Schutz, *Collected Papers*, vol. 2, *Studies in Social Theory*, edited and introduced by Arvid Brodersen (Hague: Martinus Nijoff, 1964).

CP, 3 Alfred Schutz, *Collected Papers*, vol. 3, *Studies in Phenomenological Philosophy*, edited by I. Schutz with introduction by Aron Gurwitsch (Hague: Martinus Nijhoff, 1966).

PAS *The Papers of Alfred Schutz*, Beinecke Rare Book and Manuscript Library, Yale University.

PSW Alfred Schutz, *The Phenomenology of the Social World*, translated by George Walsh and Frederick Lehnert and introduction by George Walsh (Evanston, Ill.: Northwestern University Press, 1967).

RPR Alfred Schutz, *Reflections on the Problem of Relevance*, edited, annotated, with introduction by Richard M. Zaner (New Haven: Yale University Press, 1970).

SLW Alfred Schutz and Thomas Luckmann, *The Structures of the Life-World*, translated by Richard M. Zaner and H. Tristram Engelhardt, Jr. (Evanston, Ill.: Northwestern University Press, 1973).

Preface

1. Robert Merton, "Paradigm for the Sociology of Knowledge," in *The Sociology of Knowledge: A Reader*, James E. Curtis and John W. Petras, eds. (New York and Washington: Praeger, 1970), 343.

2. Talcott Parsons, "An Approach to the Sociology of Knowledge," in *The Sociology of Knowledge: A Reader*, James E. Curtis and John W. Petras, eds. 282.

Chapter 1. The Making of the Synthesis: Schutz's Predecessors

1. Dilthey distinguishes automatic forms of *Verstehen*, which only resemble inference by analogy, and higher forms that involve a projection of oneself into a person or work on the basis of individual expressions in relation to their personal or sociohistorical contexts. Dilthey's theory of interpersonal *Verstehen* depends on his account of psychic life, the object of the *Geisteswissenschaften*, to be approached by a descriptive-analytic method, as opposed to the physical world, which is to be explored through the explanatory-synthetic method of the *Naturwissenschaften*. Dilthey's position, itself synthesizes earlier viewpoints of Windelband, who separated the *Geisteswissenschaften* from the *Naturwissenschaften* on the basis of their respective idiographic and nomothetic methods, and Rickert, who

argued that the objects of these different sciences in fact determined their methods. These early precursors of Schutz and Scheler, namely, Windelband, Rickert, and Dilthey, have not been discussed because of the limitations of time and space. Cf. Wilhelm Windelband, *Geschichte und Naturwissenschaften: Rede gehalten von dem Rektor* (Strassburg: Das Stiftungsfest der Kaiser-Wilhelms-Universität, 1894), 24, 25, 30, 36, 40; Heinrich Rickert, *Science and History: A Critique of Positivist Epistemology,* trans. George Reisman, ed. Arthur Goddard (Princeton, N.J.: Van Nostrand, 1962), 18–19, 66, 83, 102–3, 135–44; Wilhelm Dilthey, *Die geistige Welt,* ed. Georg Misch, vol. 5 of *Gesammelte Schriften* (Leipzig: B. G. Teubner and Göttingen: Vandenhoeck and Ruprecht, 1924), 211; Wilhelm Dilthey, *Descriptive Psychology and Historical Understanding,* trans. Richard M. Zaner and Kenneth L. Heiges, (Hague: Martinus Nijhoff, 1977), 4, 27–28, 42; Rudolf A. Makkreel, *Dilthey: Philosopher of the Human Sciences* (Princeton: Princeton University Press, 1975), 133.

2. *CP,* 1:159–60.

3. Ibid., 161. Cf. Max Scheler, *Formalism in Ethics and Non-formal Ethics of Values: A New Attempt toward the Formulation of an Ethical Personalism,* trans. Manfred S. Frings and Roger L. Funk (Evanston, Ill.: Northwestern University Press, 1977), 523, 525, 527, 533, 543, 558.

4. *CP,* 1:162–64.

5. Ibid., 160–61, 171–72; Cf. "Other Minds," *PAS,* B4, EI no. 6/7; spring term, 1957, 8579. Schutz's archive is divided into two sections: publications and lecture/seminar notes. The first number of an entry indicates the folder, and the letter *B* preceding a folder number shows that the folder belongs to the lecture/seminar collection. The EI number pertains to a separate numbering system within the two major sections by which the editor has indexed subsets of materials, for example, all the drafts of an individual article or a series of lectures on a common theme.

6. *CP,* 1:163. Cf. *PSW,* 23–24. Even construing a superficial attitude would involve interpretation. For instance, tears may indicate sadness or joy or a deliberate attempt to deceive the onlooker, cf. *PSW,* 27.

7. *CP,* 1:164–67.

8. Ibid., 169–72. Schutz acknowledges that the expression *stop and think* comes from John Dewey.

9. The studies mentioned are those referred to by Scheler in *The Nature of Sympathy,* trans. Peter Heath, (Hamden, Conn.: Archon Books, 1970), 238. Schutz also observes that Scheler's whole theory does not permit reflection on the self because of certain metaphysical, religious, and ethical commitments he makes about the person and his unobjectifiable character. Paradoxically, this very effort to preserve the unique, unobjectifiable character of the person prevents the possibility of self-reflection, which discloses the uniqueness of each person's stream of consciousness and undermines any possible belief in a *Gesamtperson* that might absorb individuals into itself.

10. *CP,* 1:172–75.

11. Ibid., 177–79.

12. Edmund Husserl, *Cartesian Meditations: An Introduction to Phenomenology,* trans. Dorion Cairns (Hague: Martinus Nijhoff, 1960), nos. 44–45, 92–100. *CP,* 3:58; 1:124–27, 195–97.

13. *CP,* 3:61–62.

14. Edmund Husserl, *Ideen zu einer reinen Phänomenologie und phänomenologischen Philosophie,* book 2, *Phänomenologische Untersuchungen zur Konstitu-*

tion, ed. Marly Biemel, vol. 4 of *Gesammelte Werke* (Hague: Martinus Nijhoff, 1952), no. 51, 195–96.

15. *CP,* 3:67, 73.

16. Ibid., 61–64; cf. above, 19, and "Other Minds," *PAS,* 8248. Husserl makes it clear that this assimilative apperception is not an inference by analogy involving mediating thought, but rather, as Schutz himself notes, it is a matter of almost automatic passive synthesis (Husserl, *Cartesian Meditations,* no. 50, 111). Thus, transcendental constitution would seem to involve "examining this [my livingly continuous] experience and uncovering intentionally the manner in which it bestows sense" (Husserl, *Cartesian Meditations,* no. 48, 106). Cf. Michael Theunissen, *The Other: Studies in the Social Ontology of Husserl, Heidegger, Sartre, and Buber,* trans. Christopher Macann (Cambridge and London: MIT Press, 1984), 61. Nevertheless, there still can be logical gaps of the kind Schutz is pointing out (for example, that the absolutely unique experience of my own body founds an analogical apprehension of the other's living body) in our experiential bestowing of sense. Whether such logical gaps are to be attributed to our experiential bestowing of sense or to Husserl's transcendental examination of those experiential processes, they remain logical gaps and deserve criticism. Hence, Schutz prefers to treat intersubjectivity within the framework of life worldly regularized patterns or idealizations. Maurice Natanson, *The Journeying Self: A Study in Philosophy and Social Role* (Reading, Mass.: Addison-Wesley, 1970), 32, sums up this problem:

But if the phenomenologist's effort to demonstrate how knowledge of other selves is possible is not definitive, the large question which follows is whether a proof is possible at all or whether the attempt to explore intersubjectivity by way of a proof is not mistaken in principle.

17. *CP,* 1:143; 3:71–72. Cf. José Ortega y Gasset, *Man and People,* authorized trans. R. Trask (New York: Norton, 1957), 126–27.

18. *CP,* 1:142.

19. *CP,* 3:67–69. Interestingly enough, Husserl's own transcendental procedures led to a similar conclusion by Schutz, *CP,* 3:76,

Even if one accepts Husserl's theory of constitution of the Other, according to which, by virtue of appresentative transfer, your body, appearing in my primordial sphere, leads to the constitution of your full psychic life and further to the constitution of your transcendental ego for me; even if, unlike Husserl, one admits the assumption that my appearing in your primordial sphere leads in an analogous manner to the constitution of my full psychic life and of my transcendental ego for you; if one assumes all this, still no transcendental community, no transcendental We, is ever established. On the contrary, each transcendental ego has now constituted for himself, as to its being and sense, his world, and in it all other subjects, including myself; *but* he has constituted them *just for himself and not for all other transcendental egos as well.*

CP, 3:76; cf. also 3:68–69.

20. *CP,* 3:73.

21. Ibid., 59–60. Also cf. "Scheler's Theory of Intersubjectivity, Frühe Fassung," *PAS,* 9, 1468–1740.

22. *CP,* 3:59–67.

23. Max Weber, *Economy and Society: An Outline of Interpretive Sociology,* trans.

Ephraim Fischoff and others, ed. Guenther Roth and Claus Wittich (Berkeley: University of California Press, 1978), 1:15.

24. Ibid., 4. Schutz himself devoted his attention to the interpretive under- standing of social action rather than to the causal explanation of its course and consequences. Weber's attempt to determine causes, an endeavor distinct from, but not unrelated to, interpreting subjective meaning, entailed comparative experiments. Weber explored whether the absence of alteration of certain condi- tions in situations identical with respect to all other variables might have affected the respective historical outcomes of those situations. Hence, for instance, given a similarity between late medieval conditions in China and Europe, did the lack of the Protestant ethic in China result in different economic results there five centuries later? Cf. Alexander von Schelting, *Max Webers Wissenschaftslehre: Das logische Problem der historischen Kulturerkenntnis; die Grenzen der Soziologie des Wissens* [Tübingen: J. C. B. Mohr (Paul Siebeck), 1934], 262. Certainly such an inquiry presupposes some ideal type of what subjective meaning the Protestant ethic held for its proponents. Phenomenology itself is by no means opposed to natural-scientific causal investigations that presuppose a strata of experience phenomenologically clarified. Cf. Bernhard Rang, *Kausalität und Motivation: Untersuchungen vom Verhältnis von Perspektivität und Objektivität in der Phä- nomenologie Edmund Husserls* (Hague: Martinus Nijhoff, 1973), 240. Indeed, the division of labor accomplished by the Schutzian architectonic, presented in the last chapter of this book, permits such diverse, but compatible levels of investiga- tion.

25. Weber, *Economy and Society,* 1:5–6. Cf. Max Weber, *The Methodology of the Social Sciences,* trans. and ed. Edward A. Shils and Henry A. Finch (New York: Free Press, 1949), 78–80.

26. *CP,* 1:57.

27. Weber, *Economy and Society,* 1:7.

28. Talcott Parsons, *The Structure of Social Action: A Study in Social Theory with Special Reference to a Group of Recent European Writers* (New York: Free Press, 1968), 511, 583.

29. *PSW,* 18–19. Notice that *zweckrational* actor, although he depends on *some* ultimate end for which means are chosen, as does the *wertrational* actor, is, nevertheless, willing to renegotiate even ultimate ends in a way that the *wertra- tional* actor will not. Cf. Parsons, *The Structure of Social Action,* 654.

30. Ibid., 648–49.

31. Weber, *Economy and Society,* 1:25; *PSW,* 18.

32. "Edmund Husserl," *PAS,* 15, EI no. 36, 2415.

33. "T. S. Eliot's Concept of Culture," *PAS,* 57, 11124–25. Throughout the pages of this essay on Eliot, Schutz keeps asking from whose point of view statements are being made. The punctuation in this passage is Schutz's.

34. *PSW,* 5–9.

35. *PSW,* 8. In order to take greater cognizance of the heterogeneity of the social world, Schutz specifies the various other orientations within which social relationships unfold and communication takes place. Different orientations with distinctive degrees of anonymity and temporal structures will entail different modes of communication, typification patterns, and possibilities for understand- ing. Cf. *PSW,* 8–9, 144–50.

36. *CP,* 1:210–11; *PSW,* 40.

37. Weber, *Economy and Society,* 1:8–9, 24–25; *PSW,* 26.

38. *CP,* 1:62; *PSW,* 27–29, 152, 227.

39. *CP* 2:275.

40. *PSW*, 86–96. Failure to make this distinction also prevents Weber from seeing that action affected by another, which must occur within an other-orientation, can only refer to the meaning context in which the true because motive is constituted and not to the action that is projected on the basis of because motives. That action need not occur within any other orientation at all. Such a failure keeps Weber from differentiating the diverse orientations toward others within which human action takes place. Cf. *PSW*, 147–50.

41. *PSW*, 147–50.

42. Ibid., 7.

Chapter 2. Meaning in a Social World

1. Maurice Natanson, "Phenomenology, Typification, and the World As Taken for Granted," in *Philomathēs: Studies and Essays in the Humanities in Memory of Philip Merlan*, ed. Robert B. Palmer and Robert Hamerton-Kelly (Hague: Martinus Nijhoff, 1970), 392.

2. *PSW*, 43–44, 97.

3. Natanson notes that Schutz is moving the inquirer out of the horizon of the life world and onto the terrain of transcendental phenomenology by raising questions about mundane life. Natanson argues that the possibility of thematizing the mudane from within the mundane, a possibility not questioned within phenomenological psychology, can only be considered from a transcendental level. Cf. Natanson, "Phenomenology, Typification, and the World As Taken for Granted," 392–93.

4. Aron Gurwitsch, *The Field of Consciousness* (Pittsburgh: Duquesne University Press, 1964), 403. Gurwitsch also makes the point that for the phenomenological psychologist the objects and events given in experience are still meant as existents and present themselves with a certain specific existential sense, presumably because the subjects to whom those objects are given dwell in the natural attitude and the phenomenological psychologist himself abides by the natural attitude.

5. *PSW*, 44.

6. Ibid., 44; Natanson, "Phenomenology, Typification, and the World As Taken for Granted," 392.

7. *PSW*, 44. Italics are mine.

8. Ibid., 43–44. We cannot here enter into the extensive debate about the feasibility of phenomenological reduction or about whether it can be completely enacted. If Merleau-Ponty is right, adopting reduction discloses horizons of existence beliefs and validity judgments not yet refrained from. Husserl's own employment of reduction turned up an infinite manifold of beliefs whose complete and freely executed development and presentation were not possible. Schutz's own use of reduction reveals the limits of any act of reflection that itself lies on the horizon of the object of its reflection and remains open to clarification by *later* reflective acts. In all these cases, though, uncovering the limits of reduction presupposes implementing reduction itself. Cf. Maurice Merleau-Ponty, *Phenomenology of Perception*, trans. Colin Smith (New York: Humanities Press, 1962), xiii–xiv; Edmund Husserl, *Erste Philosophie (1923/24)*, part 2, *Theorie der phänomenologischen Reduktion*, ed. Rudolf Boehm, vol. 8 of *Gesammelte Werke* (Hague: Martinus Nijhoff, 1959), 153.

9. Ibid., 45.

10. Ibid., 46–58; cf. above, 30–31. The steps taken to realize a projected act are really the act-in-progress, which Schutz technically calls *action*. The completed act, whether realized or only phantasized as such, is technically referred to as *act*.

Cox's criticism of Schutz, namely, that Schutz needs some form of reflective apprehension between reflection and lived experience, neglects the role retention plays in Schutz and weakens the contrast between lived experience and reflection that the phenomenologically inexperienced easily conflate. Cf. Ronald Cox, *Schutz's Theory of Relevance: A Phenomenological Critique* (Hague: Martinus Nijhoff, 1978), 122–23; "Bergson/James," *PAS*, B18, EI no. 19, 10851.

11. *PSW*, 56, 70, 74.

12. Ibid., 73–74. As Ricoeur points out, the later Husserl rooted theoretical activity in a more primitive power or action, thereby rethinking the sciences as a cultural activity or theoretical praxis, particularly in the *Krisis*. Cf. Paul Ricoeur, *Husserl: An Analysis of His Phenomenology*, trans. E. Ballard and L. Embree (Evanston, Ill.: Northwestern University Press, 1967), 85–86.

13. *PSW*, 69–71. Cf. Dilthey, *Descriptive Psychology and Historical Understanding*, 56–57; "On Max Scheler's Epistemology and Ethics," *PAS*, 8, EI no. 30, 1371–72.

14. *CP*, 3:97.

15. *SLW*, 233.

16. *CP*, 2:234.

17. *RPR*, 36, 122-23. In this book, Schutz notes that the ontologically pregiven structure of the world imposes itself on us in such a way that our inherited typification structures are not the only determinative factor in experience.

Habermas, too, has noted that technical and practical interests in knowledge are both grounded in deeply rooted structures of action and experience. Cf. Jürgen Habermas, *Knowledge and Interests*, trans. Jeremy J. Shapiro, 2d ed. (London: Heinemann, 1972), 371. For this reason, psychotheraphy, for instance, is always more than simply the acquisition of knowledge; therapy depends on affective-cognitive changes (cf. 287). McCarthy wonders, however, whether the later Habermas's description of the universal, transcendental conditions of speech and action derives from a whole new type of interest, since this description reflects neither technical-practical interests nor the emancipative interest that is always supposed to be directed to the concrete. Cf. Thomas McCarthy, *The Critical Theory of Jürgen Habermas* (Cambridge: MIT Press, 1978), 99–106. Perhaps the restricted number of interests that Habermas catalogs is due to his failure to grasp the structure of the underlying life world from which a diversity of interests and cognitional modes is generated.

18. *CP*, 1:21; 3:114.

19. Schutz prefers the term relevances to interests in order to avoid confining interests to the psychological, noetic side of consciousness. Human consciousness is indeed equipped with a set of relevances, or dispositions to notice, select, desire, and so on, but objects, as given, are correspondingly of relevance or impose certain relevances on the knower also.

20. *RPR*, 26–56.

21. *PSW*, 86–96. The use of the phrase *causally determined* does not refer to physical or common-sense notions of causality but rather involves bringing a motivated action and its pluperfect-tense motivating experience into a meaningful relationship. The very selection and interpretation of one meaningful experience as motivating another selected experience places us within an interpretive context that is quite different than any theory of causality based on stimulus response or the collision of inert physical objects.

It should also be noted that the breadth of possible meanings the term relevance takes on in Schutz's work suggests that the term is used in general operatively in spite of Schutz's efforts at thematic clarification. Credit for the distinction between operative and thematic concepts is due to Fink, who makes the following summary comment on the distinction:

> Let us bring our considerations together. Although Husserl, in his methodology, has inquired into the remarkable relationship that we designated as the difference between "thematic" and "operative" media of understanding, and, indeed, has to a certain extent expressly thematized this distinction in the theory of the "phenomenological reduction," the central concepts of his thought remain in the twilight. The concepts of phenomenon, epoché, constitution, performance, and transcendental logic are by far used more operatively than they are thematically clarified. They all represent problems which are still open. To see that these problems are not yet resolved is not to make an unsuitable criticism of Husserl, nor is it to overpass this thinker. The presence of a shadow is an essential feature of finite philosophizing. The more original the force which ventures to open a clearing, the deeper are the shadows which accompany basic thoughts. Only God knows without shadows. [Eugen Fink, "Operative Concepts in Husserl's Phenomenology," in *Apriori and World: European Contributions to Husserlian Phenomenology*, ed. and trans. William McKenna, Robert M. Harlan, and Laurence E. Winters (Hague: Martinus Nijhoff, 1981), 69.]

22. *PSW*, 77; *CP*, 1 : 93; *SLW*, 99–110, 122, 154–82, 222–23.

23. *SLW*, 22–24; *CP*, 1 : 207–59.

24. Schutz's limitation to a description of meaning structures, a philosophical act that is removed from immersion in mundane acts and is already a step toward the transcendental terrain, though without executing a formal phenomenological reduction, could be interpreted as an informal semireduction. Perhaps our earlier suggestion that relevance is an operative rather than thematic notion within Schutz's system is also applicable to the notion of phenomenological reduction, as Fink has point out to be true in Husserl's case.

25. *PSW*, 44, 97.

26. Ibid., 99.

27. The Bergsonian period extends from 1924 to 1928; cf. Helmut Wagner, "The Bergsonian Period of Alfred Schutz," *Philosophy and Phenomenological Research* 38 (1977): 187–99.

28. Alfred Schutz, *Life Forms and Meaning Structure*, trans., introduced, and annotated by Helmut Wagner (London: Routledge and Kegan Paul, 1982), 142.

29. This critical focus on the momentous misunderstandings possible between individuals and groups more fruitfully employs those sceptical energies in some ways misdirected toward the less practical problem of the existence of other minds. Schutz's decision to describe the natural attitude and its axiomatic positing of the Other simply bypasses the latter problem and refocuses its misspent energies.

30. *PSW*, 99.

31. Ibid., 38.

32. *CP*, 1 : 11–12; *SLW*, 59–60.

33. Ibid. Here, Schutz has resituated reflections offered by Husserl in the Fifth Cartesian Meditation within the doubly reduced sphere. There, Husserl describes how we progress beyond the diverse perspectives of our bodily posi-

tions to arrive at objective nature and a common time form. For Schutz, we achieve such commonality against the ever present horizon of individual differences often overlooked by the man in the natural attitude who relies on the general thesis of the reciprocity of perspectives.

34. *RPR*, 36; *PSW*, 108.

35. Schutz here makes use of Schleiermacher's extension of *Verstehen* beyond texts to facial gestures, speech, and so on; cf. Joachim Wach, *Das Verstehen: Grundzüge einer Geschichte der hermeneutischen Theorie im 19. Jahrhundert*, vol. 1, *Die grossen Systeme* [Tübingen: J. C. B. Mohr (Paul Siebeck), 1926–33], 92.

36. *PSW*, 108, 218; *CP*, 1:56–57.

37. This aspect of ourselves to which we are oblivious and which the Other observes corresponds to what Schutz describes elsewhere as that never reflectively grasped, nonmeaningful subjective behavior, such as unconscious physical reflexes and passive reactions, similar to Leibniz's surf of indiscernible, confused perceptions. Cf. above, 30–31.

38. *PSW*, 110–23.

39. Schutz's comments here move on an essential, philosophical plane such that in *any* communicative engagement between *any* two communicative partners, such a mutual anticipation of the meaning of the Other would take place. All three components of Schutz's methodology in *Phenomenology* (intentionality, sociality, essentiality) remain operant throughout the last three chapters of that work, even though we cannot allude to them all at the same time.

40. Ibid., 126–28, 169–70. Cf. Charles Horton Cooley, *Human Nature and the Social Order*, rev. ed. (New York: Scribners, 1922), 184. The mirroring effect is also referred to as the looking-glass effect.

41. *PSW*, 123–25. With regard to subjective meaning, Schutz contends that we can only deduce what Goethe meant by *demonic* by studying his works as a whole. Similarly, only a careful study of the history of French culture permits insight into what a French person would mean by the word *civilization*.

42. *SLW*, 282–83. It is important to note that *The Structures of the Life-World* was completed by Thomas Luckmann on the basis of plans and outlines drawn up by Schutz himself. Citations from such a work represent thought in the spirit of Schutz rather the express opinions of Schutz himself.

43. Jürgen Habermas, *Zur Logik der Sozialwissenschaften* [Tübingen: J. C. B. Mohr (Paul Siebeck), 1967], 124.

44. *CP*, 3:82.

45. Ibid., 129.

46. Natanson, *The Journeying Self*, 66.

47. *PSW*, 169.

48. Ibid., 146, 169–70; *SLW*, 62–63, 66–67.

49. *SLW*, 69.

50. *PSW*, 180–203; *SLW*, 70, 75, 80, 84.

51. *PSW*, 208–14; *SLW*, 88–92.

Chapter 3. The Distribution of Knowledge

1. *CP*, 2:121.

2. Fritz Machlup, *The Production and Distribution of Knowledge in the United States* (Princeton: Princeton University Press, 1962); Fritz Machlup, Kenneth Leeson, and others, *Information through the Printed Word: The Dissemination of Scholarly, Scientific, and Intellectual Knowledge*, 4 vols. (New York: Praeger, 1978–80). Cf. *CP*, 1:46, 118.

3. *CP*, 2 : 122–23. Cf. Fritz Machlup, *Knowledge: Its Creation, Distribution, and Economic Significance*, vol. 1, *Knowledge and Knowledge Production* (Princeton: Princeton University Press, 1980), 7–8.

4. Cf. Max Scheler, *Problems of a Sociology of Knowledge*, trans. Manfred S. Frings, ed. by Kenneth W. Stikkers (London: Routledge & Kegan Paul, 1980), 67; George H. Mead, *Mind, Self and Society, from the Standpoint of a Social Behaviorist*, ed. Charles W. Morris (Chicago: University of Chicago Press, 1934), 171. Also cf. Maurice Natanson, *The Social Dynamics of George H. Mead* (Hague: Martinus Nijhoff, 1973). Rang points out that causal investigations presuppose a phenomenological layer of appearances given to the kinaesthetic I:

> Thus it follows that relationship of the system of causality in nature, which throughout is a system of things themselves, is itself a relation of motivation in relation to the motivation context of appearances affecting the kinesthetic I. As a result, the causal system of nature can be made constitutively understandable only starting from the motivation context of appearance. [Rang, *Kausalität und Motivation*, 240.]

5. *CP*, 2 : 232–33.

6. Cf. *SLW*, 113, regarding how the combination of elements in the stock of knowledge constitutes a unique distribution of knowledge. Cf. *CP*, 2 : 120–34, 135–58; Ruth L. Horowitz, "Phenomenology and Citizenship: A Contribution by Alfred Schutz," *Philosophy and Phenomenological Research* 38 (1977): 293–311; Florian Znaniecki, *The Social Role of the Man of Knowledge* (New York: Columbia University Press, 1940).

7. *CP*, 2 : 286–87; cf. *CP*, 2 : 284; "Fragments on the Phenomenology of Music," ed. F. Kersten, *Music and Man* 2 (1976): 52. Also cf. Edmund Husserl, *Analysen zur passiven Synthesis, aus Vorlesungs- und Forschungsmanuskripten 1918–1926*, ed. Margot Fleischer, vol. 11 of *Gesammelte Werke* (Hague: Martinus Nijhoff, 1966), 25–70, 82–83, 95, 100–113.

8. Schutz agreed with Scheler and Dilthey on the continuity of consciousness. Lived experience consists in a comprehensive nexus from which reflection carves distinct meanings. Schutz observes:

> The continuity of the stream of consciousness can be explicated by a necessary relation between the emergent object of the thought and its surrounding objects. "What we hear when the thunder crashes is not thunder *pure*, but thunder-breaking-upon-silence-and-contrasting-with-it." There is no isolated object within our stream of thought, but only "substantive parts," such as sensations, perceptions, images, whose peculiarity is that they can be held before the mind for an indefinite time, and "transitive parts" which are thoughts of relations, static or dynamic, between the substantive parts. "If there be such things as feelings at all, then so surely as relations between objects exist *in rerum natura*, so surely, and more surely, do feelings exist to which these relations are known." There are, moreover, always "feelings of expectancies," of "tendencies, relating the 'present' feeling with the future and the past." In short, each of our thoughts is, so to speak, surrounded by *fringes* of not explicitly felt relations, it carries with it a "halo" of psychic overtones, or as James likes to call it, its "horizon." [*CP*, 3 : 8–9]

We have seen previously that the continuity of consciousness gives rise to the subjective meaning of an expression, its fringe, the aura of psychological associations accruing to every objective meaning of a sign. Cf. above, 43–44.

9. *PSW*, 60–64; *RPR*, 112–13; *CP*, 2 : 288–91.

10. *PSW*, 98–99. Cf. Maurice Natanson, *Edmund Husserl: Philosopher of Infinite Tasks* (Evanston, Ill.: Northwestern University Press, 1973), 113–14.

11. *PSW*, 178–84.

12. *CP*, 2:111–12.

13. Ibid., 114.

14. *SLW*, 48–58; Edmund Husserl, *The Phenomenology of Internal Time-Consciousness*, ed. Martin Heidegger, trans. James S. Churchill (Bloomington: Indiana University Press, 1964), 97.

15. The idealization of the reciprocity of perspectives extends to higher level cognitive activities beyond perception also, activities by which we gain access to knowledge formerly inaccessible to us simply by consulting another. Cf. Husserl, *Analysen zur passiven Synthesis*, 25.

16. *CP*, 2:112.

17. Ibid., 128–29.

18. *CP*, 2:95. Cf. above, 44–45.

19. *CP*, 2:104.

20. *CP*, 2:96, 100–101, 103, 249. Cf. Max Scheler, *Die Wissensformen und die Gesellschaft* (Leipzig: Der Neue Geist, 1926), 313, 401, 428, 484; Max Scheler, *Schriften zur Soziologie und Weltanschauungslehre;* vol. 1, *Moralia*, 7; vol. 2, *Nation und Weltanschauung*, 12, 14; vol. 3, *Christentum und Gesellschaft*, 20, 23, 50 (Leipzig: P. Reinhold, 1923); Scheler, *Problems of a Sociology of Knowledge*, 47, 67, 69, 70, 73, 74, 98, 103, 113, 119, 168.

21. *CP*, 2:260.

22. Ibid.

23. Ibid., 98, 133, 246–47; above, 39.

24. *CP*, 2:131–33.

25. Ibid.,133. Schutz borrows the "relatively natural concept of the world" from Scheler; cf. Scheler, *Problems of a Sociology of Knowledge*, 74.

26. Above, 52.

27. Jürgen Habermas, *Communication and the Evolution of Society*, trans. Thomas McCarthy (London: Heinemann, 1976), 178–86, 193–94, 197; cf. also Paul Connerton, ed. *Critical Sociology: Selected Readings* (New York: Penguin, 1976), 367, 388.

28. *CP*, 2:254. Cf. Georg Simmel, *The Web of Group Affiliations*, trans. Reinhard Bendix (New York: Free Press, 1955), 140–41. In that passage, Simmel compares the object that is a synthesis of perceptions with the individual who is a synthesis of diverse social groups in which he participates, thereby bringing into relationship phenomenology and Simmel's unique brand of sociology.

29. Adorno concurs:

> Rather, it would appear that sociological factors play an essential but *complex and indirect* psychological role. Social psychology must, therefore, advance beyond its initial stage of seeking—and expecting to find—simple relationships between ideology and group membership; it must go on to study the complex processes by which the individual *selectivity assimilates* the manifold pressures from his socioideological environment.[T. W. Adorno and others, *The Authoritarian Personality* (New York: Norton, 1950), 206.]

Of course, that individual selectivity is itself sociohistorically shaped for Schutz.

30. *PSW*, 97.

Chapter 4. The Distribution of Knowledge as Protosociology

1. *CP*, 1:116–17.
2. Ibid., 130–31.
3. Ibid., 122, 131–32; *CP*, 3:38–39; above, 20, 24.
4. *CP*, 1:141–42. Max Scheler, toward the end of his life, formulated his own philosophical anthropology in *Man's Place in Nature*, trans. Hans Meyerhoff (Boston: Beacon, 1961), 3–7, 88–95.
5. By this socialization of typification patterns, Schutz has contributed significantly to the phenomenology *and the sociology* of typifications, according to Helmut Wagner, *Alfred Schutz: An Intellectual Biography* (Chicago: University of Chicago Press, 1983), 293.
6. Merleau-Ponty also points out the close bond between philosophy and sociology:

> Thus philosophy is not defined by a particular domain of its own. Like sociology, it only speaks about the world, men and mind. It is distinguished by a certain *mode* of consciousness we have of others, of nature, or of ourselves. It is nature and man in the present, not "flattened out" (Hegel) in a derivative objectivity but such as they are presented in our present cognitive and active commerce with them. Philosophy is nature in us, the others in us, and we in them. Accordingly, we must not simply say that philosophy is compatible with sociology, but that it is necessary to it as a constant reminder of its tasks; and that each time the sociologist returns to the living sources of his knowledge, to what operates within him as a means of understanding the forms of culture most remote from him, he practices philosophy spontaneously. Philosophy is not a particular body of knowledge; it is the vigilance which does not let us forget the source of all knowledge. [Maurice Merleau-Ponty, "The Philosopher and Sociology," in *Signs*, trans. Richard C. McCleary (Evanston: Ill. North-western University Press, 1964), 110.]

7. Cf. Schutz's criticism of Fink's paradoxes in *CP*, 1:257–59; 3:83; Eugen Fink, "The Phenomenological Philosophy of Edmund Husserl and Contemporary Criticism," in *The Phenomenology of Husserl: Selected Critical Readings*, ed. and trans. R. O. Elveton (Chicago: Quadrangle, 1970), 105–6, 143–44; Jacques Derrida, *Speech and Phenomena, and Other Essays on Husserl's Theory of Signs*, trans. David B. Allison (Evanston, Ill.: Northwestern University Press, 1973), 50–51; Michael Foucault, *The Archeology of Knowledge*, trans. A. M. Sheridan Smith (New York: Harper and Row, 1972), 209–10; Michael Foucault, *The Order of Things, an Archeology of the Human Sciences* (New York: Pantheon, 1970), 322–23; cf. Suzanne Cunningham, *Language and the Phenomenological Reductions of Edmund Husserl* (Hague: Martinus Nijhoff, 1976), 73–75.
8. *CP*, 1:12; 3:131. Cf. Edmund Husserl, *Phenomenological Psychology*, trans. John Scanlon (Hague: Martinus Nijhoff, 1977), 112.
Habermas's insistence that the confirmation of behavior toward objects (objectivity of experience) be kept separate from the successful justification of propositions within discourse (claims to truth), while an important reminder of the difference between levels, overlooks the continuity that Husserl saw clearly between basic perceptual anticipations, which are "verified," and higher level scientific hypotheses. Cf. Jürgen Habermas, "Wahrheitstheorien," *Wirklichkeit und Reflexion: Walter Schulz zum 60. Geburtstag*, ed. Helmut Fahrenbach (Pfullingen: Neske, 1973), 233–34. Cf. *PSW*, 221; Edmund Husserl, *Experience*

and Judgment: Investigations in a Genealogy of Logic, trans. James S. Churchill and Karl Ameriks (Evanston, Ill.: Northwestern University Press, 1973), 203–4, 251.

9. *PSW* 124–25.

10. *CP,* 2:275; above, 32.

11. *PSW,* 135.

12. Social science involves a specific type of intersubjective understanding within the broader framework of intersubjective understanding in the life world. Cf. *CP,* 1:55–62. Hence, *Phenomenology* forms a background for social-scientific understanding.

13. Above, 26.

14. *CP,* 1:62–66; cf. Ernest Nagel, "Symposium: Problems of Concept and Theory Formation in Social Sciences," in *Science, Language, and Human Rights,* vol. 1, [*Proceedings of*]*American Philosophical Association, Eastern Division,* (Philadelphia: University of Pennsylvania Press, 1952), 56, 60, 63.

15. *PSW,* 222.

16. *CP,* 1:37, 39, 62–63; "Das Problem der Personalität in der Sozialwelt," EI no. 20, 49.5; "Die Welt des Traumes," *PAS,* 7198.

17. "Das Problem der Personalität in der Sozialwelt," *PAS,* 7200–7201.

18. *CP,* 1:63.

19. By contrast, the historian investigates unique occurrences, according to Schutz. Economics offers abundant examples of lawlike, clarifying, typical constructs that present "the typical and invariant subjective experiences of anyone who acts within the economic framework." *PSW,* 245.

20. *CP,* 1:60, 63–64.

21. Ibid., 52–55. Cf. Maurice Natanson, *Literature, Philosophy, and the Social Sciences: Essays in Existentialism and Phenomenology* (Hague: Martinus Nijhoff, 1962), 166.

22. *CP,* 1:56.

23. Ibid., 43–44.

24. Above, 67.

25. *CP,* 1:116–17. We judge social-scientific descriptions to be actually clarificatory if they fulfill the three postulates Schutz developed in response to Nagel's call for verification.

26. "Bergson/James," *PAS,* B18, EI no. 19, 10851.

27. Because this reflective turn toward experience also takes place outside the formal scientific attitude, there is a sense in which we are already social scientists in the life world when we reflect in our own lived experience and that of others. "For in a certain sense, I am a social scientist in everyday life whenever I reflect upon my fellow men and their behavior instead of merely experiencing them." *PSW,* 140.

Likewise, the sociologist in reflecting on his experience becomes a kind of philosopher, according to Merleau-Ponty: "The sociologist philosophizes every time he is required to not only record but comprehend the facts. At the moment of interpretation, he is himself already a philosopher." (Merleau-Ponty, "The Philosopher and Sociology," 101.)

28. Above, 111.

29. *PSW,* 241.

30. *CP,* 1:257.

31. Above, 36.

32. Cf. Merleau-Ponty, *Phenomenology of Perception,* xiii–xiv; *CP,* 1:210; *PSW,* 70–71, 74. Cf. Husserl, *Erste Philosophie,* part 2, 153.

33. The scientific *epoché* is responsible for the social situation resembling that of the indirect social observation of contemporaries. We do not first assume a they orientation and then execute *epoché;* the they orientation follows on the *epoché.*

34. The postulate of adequacy springs from a laudable scepticism about the self-containedness of social science. Schutz is well aware of the social character of social science itself, its tendency to define problems and project solutions according to socially approved patterns that might affect data collection (above, 67–68). Hence, the postulates of adequacy and subjective interpretation posit a dialectical counterpole to the social scientist's personal and social position and the particular distribution of knowledge it fixes. For a particularly insightful illustration of the challenge that the postulate of adequacy poses to social science; cf. Bënetta Jules-Rosette, "The Veil of Objectivity: Prophecy, Divination, and Social Inquiry," *American Anthropologist* 80 (1978):549–70. Ms. Jules-Rosette describes her effort to pursue anthropology by becoming a church member within an indigenous African church. She shows that within ethnographic studies, the social scientist's own preconceptions need to be confronted while he inquires into the Other. The social scientist, in Jules-Rosette's view, ends up finally being judged by the layperson also.

The social scientist, on the other hand, can also see things that the actors he studies do not see or even refuse to see due to ideological factors. This possibility suggests that Schutz's postulate of adequacy, namely, that the typical scientific construct be "understandable for the actor himself," must be considered in a more complex dialogical-hermeneutical fashion.

35. The final comments of "Concept and Theory Formation in the Social Sciences" provide instances of how scientific purposes can be met in spite of incomplete understandings. According to those comments, certain determinate relations between a set of variables can be discovered, and ascertainable regularities can be explained (*CP*, 1:64–65). Predictions about how an individual or group will behave can be fulfilled through empirical regularities even though failures to understand remain latent.

Chapter 5. The Distribution of Knowledge as Protophilosophy

1. Much of this section of Chapter 5 borrows from the article "Constitution and the Sedimentation of the Social in Alfred Schutz's Theory of Typification," by Michael D. Barber, in *The Modern Schoolman* 54 (1987), 111–120.

2. Edmund Husserl, *Ideen zu einer reinen Phänomenologie*, book 2, xv.

3. *CP*, 3:17.

4. *Ideen zu einer reinen Phänomenologie*, book 2, 21.

5. Ibid., 27–32, 38, 54, 130–31.

6. Edmund Husserl, *Ideen zu einer reinen Phänomenologie und phänomenologischen Philosophie*, book 1, *Allgemeine Einfuhrung in die reine Phänomenologie*, ed. Karl Schuhmann, vol. 3 of *Gesammelte Werke* (Hague: Martinus Nijhoff, 1976), 86; cf. *Ideas Pertaining to a Pure Phenomenology and to a Phenomenological Philosophy*, book 1, *General Introduction to a Pure Phenomenology*, trans. F. Kersten (Hague: Martinus Nijhoff, 1982), 88–89.

7. Husserl to Dilthey, 29 June 1911, "Correspondencia entre Dilthey y Husserl," *Revista de Filosofía de la Universidad de Costa Rica* 1 (1957):114.

8. Cf. Edmund Husserl, *Erfahrung und Urteil: Untersuchungen zur Genealogie*

der Logik, ed. Ludwig Landgrebe (Prag: Acadamia, 1939), 20, regarding sedimented *(niedergeschlagen)* layers; cf. Husserl, *Experience and Judgment,* 26.

9. *CP,* 1:10–15; 2:95.

10. *CP,* 3:115.

11. Ibid., 100.

12. Ibid., 107.

13. Ibid., 108.

14. *CP,* 1:114.

15. *CP,* 3:107.

16. Ibid., 108.

17. That is, in the case of eidetically elaborated universal structures.

18. Husserl, *Phenomenological Psychology,* 116.

19. *CP,* 3:114–115.

20. Ibid., 115.

21. The previous two quotations speak of both the *object* experienced and the *type* in terms of which we experience the object, that type, of course, being socially derived. Are the essential characteristics illuminated by eidetic analysis determined by the ontology of the object or the society passing on the types? Perhaps eidetic analysis really makes manifest the necessary characteristics constituting what is given in experience without having to determine what proportion of the type of object is ontologically derived and what proportion sociologically derived. Instead of viewing these social or ontological sources as being in competition, they can function symbiotically, as Barnes has suggested. Cf. Barry Barnes, "On the Conventional Character of Knowledge and Cognition," *Philosophy of the Social Sciences* 11 (1981): 318.

22. Cf. Fred Kersten, "Phenomenology, History, Myth" in *Phenomenology and Social Reality: Essays in Memory of Alfred Schutz,* ed. Maurice Natanson (Hague: Martinus Nijhoff, 1970), 268–69:

> In this sense, preserving the full access to the sub-scientific dimension of the world is the pre-condition for scientific interpretation of the world. Indeed, we may now say that all typifications, empirical or pure, hence all categorialization and conceptualization, philosophic and scientific or not, bears a constitutive reference to the "Logos of the aesthetic world" which shapes, guides and warrants that typification, categorialization and conceptualization (although, to be sure, it does not establish their validity).

23. *CP,* 3:110.

24. *PSW,* 130–31.

25. Ibid., 130.

26. Ibid., 93.

27. Schutz uses the example of a question-and-answer situation, *PSW,* 159–63.

28. Kripke has advanced an interesting and related argument in his essay "Identity and Necessity." Kripke makes the case that the statement "Heat is the motion of molecules" can stand as a necessary identity statement. It possesses the "illusion of contingency" because it is discoverable to us who are sensitive to heat in a way that Martians, for instance, are not. Martians might not have the sensation of heat when touching objects that are hot to us because of their particular neural structures. But, for Kripke, "giving off a particular kind of sensation" is a contingent property of heat and not a rigid designator playing a definitional role, as motion of molecules does in relation to heat. Kripke contends that the adjectives *necessary* and *contingent* pertain to metaphysics, whereas

a priori and *a posteriori* are epistemological properties. We, then, must distinguish between a necessary truth and the sociohistorical process through which that truth is acquired. It seems to me that the distinction between, on the one hand, the validity of an eidetic statement that affirms certain necessary relationships and, on the other hand, the social process through which that claim was fashioned and acquired repeats distinctions analogous to those which Kripke is drawing. We can reach a necessary truth through a particular socially conditioned process, but that does not mean that the statement investigated about how it came to be cannot claim necessity. Cf. Saul Kripke, "Identity and Necessity," in *Naming, Necessity, and Natural Kinds,* ed. Stephen P. Schwartz (Ithaca, N.Y.: Cornell University Press, 1977), 84–85, 95–98.

29. *PSW,* 95.

Chapter 6. The Distribution of Knowledge and the Sociology of Knowledge

1. Much of the first section of Chapter 6 borrows from an article by Michael D. Barber, "Alfred Schutz's Methodology and the Paradox of the Sociology of Knowledge," *Philosophy Today,* 30 (1986): 58–65.

2. Above, 77–80.

3. Ernst Grünwald, *Das Problem der Soziologie des Wissens: Versuch einer kritischen Darstellung der wissenssoziologischen Theorien* (Wien-Leipzig: Wilhelm Braumüller, 1934), 229.

4. Merleau-Ponty, "The Philosopher and Sociology," 109.

5. Habermas, "Wahrheitstheorien," 218, 226–28; Edmund Husserl, *Logical Investigations,* trans. J. N. Findlay (New York: Humanities Press, 1970), 760, 762, 764–65; J. N. Mohanty, *The Possibility of Transcendental Philosophy* (Dordrecht, Boston, Lancaster: Martinus Nijhoff, 1985), 92, 214.

6. Cf. David Bloor, *Knowledge and Social Imagery* (London and Boston: Routledge and Kegan Paul, 1976), 14; similarly, Barnes remarks:

This idea of competition between what is logical and natural on the one hand, and what derives from culture and society on the other, is deeply entrenched. Classifications may conform to the objective facts of nature *or* to cultural requirements. They may be logical or social. But this is the very opposite of what a careful analysis reveals: we need to think in terms of *symbiosis,* not competition. [Barnes, "On the Conventional Character of Knowledge and Cognition," 318.]

7. Above, 85–87.

8. Of course, the very fact that we are discussing validity criteria indicates the presence of some kind of scientific viewpoint beyond lived experience in which validity criteria are not reflected on. Since most scientific viewpoints do not, however, entail phenomenological reduction, but rather proceed within the natural attitude, Schutz's account of the life world with its socially conditioned intentional structures would apply to them also.

9. Husserl comments:

He [the naturalist] is, however, an idealist who sets up and (so he thinks) justifies theories, which deny precisely what he presupposes in his idealistic way of acting, whether it be in constructing theories or in justifying and recommending values or practical norms as the most beautiful and the best.

He is, after all, going on presuppositions, to the extent that he theorizes at all, to the extent that he objectively sets up values to which value judgments are to correspond, and likewise in setting up any practical rules according to which each one is to be guided in his willing and his conduct. The naturalist teaches, preaches, moralizes, reforms. (Häckel and Ostwald are good examples.) But he denies what every sermon, every demand, if it is to have a meaning presupposes. The only thing is, he does not preach in express terms that the only rational thing to do is to deny reason, as well theoretical as axiological and practical reason. He would, in fact, banish that sort of thing far from him. The absurdity is not in his case evident, but remains hidden from him because he naturalizes reason. [Edmund Husserl, *Philosophy As Rigorous Science*, in *Phenomenology and the Crisis of Philosophy*, trans. Quentin Lauer (New York: Harper and Row, 1965), 81.]

10. Karl Marx, "Contribution to the Critique of Hegel's Philosophy of Right," in *Early Writings*, trans. and ed. T. B. Bottomore (New York: McGraw-Hill, 1964), 44. Cf. Karl Marx, "Zur Kritik der Hegelschen Rechtsphilosophie," in Karl Marx, Friedrich Engels, *Werke* (Berlin: Dietz Verlag, 1962), 1:379.

11. Karl Marx and Friedrich Engels, *The German Ideology: A Critique of the Most Recent German Philosophy As Represented by Feuerbach, B. Bauer, and Stirner*, in *Writings of the Young Marx on Philosophy and Society*, ed. and trans. Loyd D. Easton and Kurt H. Guddat (Garden City, N.Y.: Anchor, 1967), 406–407. Cf. Karl Marx and Friedrich Engels, *Die deutsche Ideologie*, in *Werke*, 3:26–27; cf. also 17–77, 176, 227, 263, 274–75 in the German edition.

12. Karl Marx, preface to *A Contribution to the Critique of Political Economy* in Karl Marx and Friedrich Engels, *Selected Works* (New York: International Publishers, 1968), 182–83; Cf. vorwort, *Zur Kritik der politischen Ökonomie*, in *Werke*, 13:9. Marx's comments on natural science suggest Habermas's discussion of Marx's scientism in *Knowledge and Human Interests*, 46.

13. Marx and Engels, *The German Ideology*, 414–15; *Die deutsche Ideologie*, 26–27.

14. For a discussion of how the term ideology, originally the study of ideas in the work of Destutt de Tracy and others, gradually acquired its pejorative meaning in Marx, precisely because that study was undertaken without regard for the socioeconomic underpinnings of ideas, cf. Emmet Kennedy, *A Philosophe in the Age of Revolution: Destutt de Tracy and the Origins of "Ideology"* (Philadelphia: American Philosophical Society, 1978), 339–46.

15. Grünwald, 62. Cf. Habermas, *Knowledge and Human Interests*, 42, on Marx's inattention to the structures of symbolic action and the role of cultural traditions so that he could focus on labor and production relationships.

16. G. W. F. Hegel, *Philosophy of Right*, trans. T. M. Knox (London: Oxford University Press, 1967), 217; Grünwald, 28, 35–36; Friedrich Engels, *Ludwig Feuerbach and the End of Classical German Philosophy*, in *Selected Works* (New York: International Publishers, 1968), 619; *Ludwig Feuerbach und der Ausgang der klassischen deutschen Philosophie*, in *Werke* (Berlin: Dietz Verlag, 1962), 21:277, 292–93.

17. Merton, "Paradigm for the Sociology of Knowledge," 343; above, 9; Alexander von Schelting, *Max Weber's Wissenschaftslehre*, 114.

18. Talcott Parsons, "An Approach to the Sociology of Knowledge," in *The Sociology of Knowledge: A Reader*, James E. Curtis and John W. Petras, eds. (New York and Washington: Praeger, 1970), 282; Werner Stark, *The Sociology of Knowledge: An Essay in Aid of a Deeper Understanding of the History of Ideas* (Glencoe, Ill.:

Free Press, 1958), 284; Engels to C. Schmidt, 27 Oct. 1890, *Selected Works* (New York: International Publishers, 1968), 697–98; Engels to F. Merhring, 14 July 1893, 701; Engels to W. Borgius, 25 Jan. 1894, 704. Cf. Engels, *Briefe*, in *Werke* (Berlin: Dietz, 1956–68), 37: 491–93; 39:96–98, 205–6. Cf. Engels to Joseph Block, 21 Sept. 1890, *Werke* 37:463–65; Engels to Conrad Schmidt, 5 Aug. 1890, 37:436. In all these letters, Engels argues for reciprocating relations of determinism between substructure and superstructure, with a priority given to economic determinisms.

19. Grünwald on Adler, 143; Frank Hartung, "Problems of the Sociology of Knowledge," in *The Sociology of Knowledge: A Reader*, James E. Curtis and John W. Petras, eds. (New York and Washington: Praeger, 1970), 687–88.

20. K. Danziger, "Ideology and Utopia in South Africa: A Methodological Contribution to the Sociology of Knowledge," in *Towards the Sociology of Knowledge: Origin and Development of a Sociological Thought Style*, ed Gunter W. Remmling (London: Routledge and Kegan Paul, 1973), 364.

21. Grünwald, 157. Scheler consistently opposed the view that cultural phenomena could be deduced from particular social relationships; cf. Scheler, *Problems of a Sociology of Knowledge*, 38, 53–54, 173.

22. Deena Weinstein and Michael A. Weinstein, "The Sociology of Nonknowledge: A Paradigm," in *Research in Sociology of Knowledge, Sciences and Art: An Annual Compilation of Research*, ed. Robert Alun Jones (Greenwich, Conn.: Jai Press, 1978), 1:160–61.

23. Grünwald, 196–97; Stark, 141, 148; Irving Louis Horowitz, *Philosophy, Science and the Sociology of Knowledge* (Springfield, Ill.: Charles C. Thomas, 1961), 9.

24. Grünwald, 153; Schelting, 114–16; Engels, above, 116–17n.18.

25. Scheler, *Problems of a Sociology of Knowledge*, 36, *passim*.

26. Weber, *The Methodology of the Social Sciences*, 45, 68–69, 73, 80, 88, 173, 185, 186; Max Weber, *From Max Weber: Essays in Sociology*, trans. and ed. H. H. Gerth and C. Wright Mills (New York: Oxford University Press, 1946), 268, 284, 323–24; cf. the whole of Max Weber, *The Protestant Ethic and the Spirit of Capitalism*, trans. Talcott Parsons (New York: Scribners, 1958); Schelting, 114–16.

27. Karl Mannheim, *Ideology and Utopia: An Introduction to the Sociology of Knowledge*, trans. Louis Wirth and Edward Shils (London: Kegan Paul, Trench, Trubner, and Co., 1936), 241, 252, 256; Karl Mannheim, *Essays on the Sociology of Knowledge*, ed. and trans. Paul Kecskemeti (New York: Oxford University Press, 1952), 96–97, 128, 176; Karl Mannheim, *Structures of Thinking*, ed. David Kettler, Volker Meja, and Nico Stehr; trans. Jeremy J. Shapiro and Shierry Weber Nicholsen (London: Routledge and Kegan Paul, 1982), 55, 72, 88, 93, 96–97, 122, 220, 266, 270.

28. Robert K. Merton, "Paradigm for the Sociology of Knowledge," in *The Sociology of Knowledge: A Reader*, 343; Robert K. Merton, *Social Theory and Social Structure*, rev. and enl. ed. (Glencoe, Ill.: Free Press, 1957), 441, 463; Robert K. Merton, *The Sociology of Science: Theoretical and Empirical Investigations*, ed. Norman W. Storer (Chicago and London: University of Chicago Press, 1973), 49, 65.

29. Parsons, "An Approach to the Sociology of Knowledge," in *The Sociology of Knowledge: A Reader*, 282; Parsons, *The Structure of Social Action*, 765.

30. *CP*, 1:62–63.

31. Ibid., 2:84–85.

32. *PSW*, 241–49.

33. Wolff's charge that Schutz tends not to pay attention to how the range of

our interests is socially circumscribed in advance and how we are thus prone to forms of false consciousness overlooks the architectonic setting in which Schutz's own work must be placed in relation to level-three investigations. Further, the notion of the distribution of knowledge and the resultant diversity of perspectives that make possible mutual criticism provides a valuable tool for explaining false consciousness and the processes of its unmasking. Cf. Kurt H. Wolff, "Discussion of Wagner, Imber, and Rasmussen" in *Alfred Schutz: Appraisals and Developments*, ed. Kurt H. Wolff (Dordrecht: Martinus Nijhoff, 1984), 30–32. This book is a reprint of *Human Studies*, vol. 7, no. 2 (1984), the entire issue of which is devoted to Schutz.

34. This discussion of levels is in no way meant to refer to the old unity-of-the-sciences project to reduce all sciences to physics. Rather, each level possesses its own distinctive and legitimate problems and methods.

Weinstein and Weinstein argue that the work of Peter Berger and Thomas Luckmann, both followers of Schutz, tends to "stress the primacy of face-to-face relations" and so "marginalize those who critique the social system as a whole." Cf. Deena Weinstein and Michael Weinstein, "Sociologies of Knowledge as Rhetorical Strategies," *Free Inquiry* 6 (1978):11–13. Such a criticism, if applied to Schutz, would overlook the locus of Schutz's efforts within his own architectonic.

Berger and Luckmann deserve some discussion, since their *The Social Construction of Reality* insightfully related Schutz's thought to the sociology of knowledge for the first time. In that book, the authors deny they are writing a philosophical treatise. Rather, they describe the everyday life world and then offer an account of the sociological mechanisms, such as institutionalization, legitimation, and internalization, by which that life world is sociologically established [cf. *The Social Construction of Reality: A Treatise in the Sociology of Knowledge* (Garden City, N.Y.: Doubleday, 1966), 12–13]. The preeminent achievement of Berger and Luckmann, in my opinion, is their realization that the sociology of knowledge, traditionally preoccupied with only the social and economic determination of highly organized fields of knowledge within a culture (for example, law, philosophy, art, religion), can and ought to devote itself to an analysis of "everything that passes for 'knowledge' in society" (Ibid., 13). Just as Schutz made the life world, with its everyday typifications and recipes for action, a theme of philosophical investigation, so Berger and Luckmann have shown that the same domain is open to examination by the sociology of knowledge. My work, however, tries to address some of the philosophical, epistemological, and methodological questions that Berger and Luckmann deliberately set aside. Furthermore, understanding the philosophical character of Schutz's work would blunt the criticisms the Weinsteins are making here, for Schutz's purpose is to lay the philosophical foundations that traditional sociologists of knowledge ignore or presuppose. Properly situating Schutz's achievement within the broad architectonic it founds opens up a diversity of possible sociological approaches and prevents the absolutization of any one mode of analysis. To my knowledge, neither Schutz nor Berger and Luckmann have argued that one form of sociological analysis takes precedence over all others.

35. George C. Homans, "Bringing Men Back In," in *The Philosophy of Social Explanation*, ed. Alan Ryan (London: Oxford University Press, 1973), 51, 55, 59–63.

36. Emile Durkheim, *The Rules of Sociological Method*, 8th ed., trans. Sarah A. Solvay and John H. Mueller and ed. by George E. G. Catlin (Glencoe, Ill.: Free Press, 1958), 58; Homans, 52.

37. Anthropologist Geertz argues that there is less danger of simplistic reductionism if we examine cultural expressions as texts of meaning rather than as mere effects of social mechanics.

> The culture of a people is an ensemble of texts, themselves ensembles, which the anthropologist strains to read over the shoulders of those to whom they properly belong. There are enormous difficulties in such an enterprise, methodological pitfalls to make a Freudian quake, and some moral perplexities as well. Nor is it the only way that symbolic forms can be sociologically handled. Functionalism lives, and so does psychologism. But to regard such forms as "saying something of something," and saying it to somebody, is at least to open up the possibility of an analysis which attends to their substance rather than to reductive formulas professing to account for them. [Clifford Geertz, *The Interpretation of Cultures: Selected Essays* (New York: Basic Books, 1973), 452–53.]

38. Above, 94.

39. *CP*, 1:92; cf. Henri Bergson, *Time and Free Will: An Essay on the Immediate Data of Consciousness,* trans. F. L. Pogson (London: George Allen and Unwin and New York: The Macmillan Company, 1950), 175–92; cf. *Essai sur les Données Immédiates de la Conscience* (Paris: F. Alcan, 1889), 134–47.

40. Above, 73–74.

41. For Durkheim, even the highly individualistic act of suicide and the individualistic mentality conducive to it were themselves the product of *social* factors, namely, the *conscience collective* of Protestantism in which neither Catholics nor Jews shared. Cf. Emile Durkheim, *Suicide: A Study in Sociology,* trans. John A. Spaulding and George Simpson (Glencoe, Ill.: Free Press, 1951), 152–70; cf. also Parsons, *The Structure of Social Action*, 334.

42. Georg Simmel, *The Web of Group Affiliations,* trans. Richard Bendix (New York: Free Press, 1955), 140–41.

43. *CP*, 2:121; above, 49.

Bibliography

The following bibliography contains the complete published works of Alfred Schutz as well as a select, annotated bibliography of his unpublished materials as found in *The Papers of Alfred Schutz*, held by the Beinecke Rare Book and Manuscript Library, Yale University. This bibliography does not include an exhaustive list of articles and books about Schutz, but only those relevant to the place of sociology of knowledge in Schutz's thought. Finally, only works cited in this book and those closely associated with the topic of this book are mentioned under Related Works.

Works by Schutz

BOOKS, ARTICLES, REVIEWS

Collected Papers. Vol. 1, *The Problem of Social Reality.* Edited by Maurice Natanson. Hague: Martinus Nijhoff, 1962.

Collected Papers. Vol. 2, *Studies in Social Theory.* Edited by Arvid Brodersen. Hague: Martinus Nijhoff, 1964

Collected Papers. Vol. 3, *Studies in Phenomenological Philosophy.* Edited by I. Schutz. Hague: Martinus Nijhoff, 1966.

"Felix Kaufmann, 1895–1949." *Social Research* 17 (1950):1–7.

"Fragments on the Phenomenology of Music." Edited by F. Kersten. *Music and Man* 2 (1976):5–71.

Introduction to "Husserl's Importance for the Social Sciences." In *Edmund Husserl: 1859–1957,* edited by H. L. Van Breda and J. Taminiaux. Hague: Martinus Nijhoff, 1959.

"Kurt Riezler." A memorial notice written with Horace M. Kallen. *Proceedings and Addresses of the American Philosophical Association* 30 (1957): 114–15.

On Phenomenology and Social Relations: Selected Writings. Edited by Helmut R. Wagner. Chicago and London: University of Chicago Press, 1970.

Reflections on the Problem of Relevance. Edited by Richard M. Zaner. New Haven: Yale University Press, 1970.

Reply to Charles W. Morris's comment on "Symbol, Reality, and Society." In *Symbols and Society,* edited by Lyman Bryson, Louis Finkelstein, Hudson Hoagland, and R. M. MacIver. New York: Harper, 1955.

Review of *The Foundation of Phenomenology* by Marvin Farber. *Philosophical Abstracts* 3 (1944):8–9.

Review of *Formale und transzendentale Logik* by Edmund Husserl. *Deutsche Literaturzeitung* 54 (1933): 773–84.

Review of *Méditations Cartésiennes* by Edmund Husserl. *Deutsche Literaturzeitung* 53 (1932): 2404–16.

Der sinnhafte Aufbau der sozialen Welt: eine Einleitung in die verstehende Soziologie. Vienna: Springer, 1932. Translated by George Walsh and Frederick Lehnert

120

under the title *The Phenomenology of the Social World*. Evanston, Ill.: Northwestern University Press, 1967.

Theorie der Lebensformen. Frankfurt am Main: Suhrkamp, 1981. Edited and translated by Helmut Wagner under the title *Life Forms and Meaning Structure*. London: Routledge and Kegan Paul, 1982.

"Tomoo Otakas Grundlegung der Lehre vom sozialen Verband." *Zeitschrift für öffentliches Recht* 17 (1937): 64–84.

COLLABORATIONS

Schutz, Alfred, and Aron Gurwitsch. *Briefwechsel 1939–1959*. Edited by Richard Grathoff. Munich: Wilhelm Fink Verlag, 1986. Forthcoming translation by Claude Evans under the title *Schutz-Gurwitsch Correspondence 1939–1959*. Bloomington: Indiana University Press, 1987.

Schutz, Alfred, and Thomas Luckmann. *Strukturen der Lebenswelt*. Vol. 1. Neuwied: Luchterhand, 1975. Translated by Richard M. Zaner and H. Tristram Engelhardt, Jr., under the title *The Structures of the Lifeworld*. Evanston, Ill.: Northwestern University Press, 1975.

———. *Strukturen der Lebenswelt*. Vol. 2. Frankfurt am Main: Suhrkamp, 1984.

Schutz, Alfred, and Talcott Parsons. *Zur Theorie sozialen Handelns: Briefwechsel/ Alfred Schütz, Talcott Parsons*. Frankfurt am Main: Suhrkamp, 1977. Edited and translated by Richard Grathoff under the title *The Theory of Social Action: The Correspondence of Alfred Schutz and Talcott Parsons*. Bloomington: Indiana University Press, 1978.

EDITED MANUSCRIPTS

Schutz, Alfred, ed. "Notizen zur Raumkonstitution" by Edmund Husserl. *Philosophy and Phenomenological Research* 1 (1940): 21–27, 217–26.

———, ed. "Die Welt der lebendigen Gegenwart und die Konstitution der äusserleiblichen Umwelt" by Edmund Husserl. *Philosophy and Phenomenological Research* 6 (1946):323–43.

UNPUBLISHED WORKS

The Papers of Alfred Schutz in the Beinecke Rare Book and Manuscript Library at Yale University contains over eleven thousand pages consisting of two parts: (1) a collection of published and unpublished manuscripts, totaling about 7,600 pages, one-third of which are in German; and (2) a collection of notes from lectures and seminars that Schutz gave at the New School for Social Research. The majority of these materials is handwritten, although the manuscript section regularly includes two or three handwritten rough drafts of many of the articles in *Collected Papers*, with the final copy being typewritten. The lecture and seminar files comprise course plans, reading lists, and notes on various authors read during the courses, including Schutz's responses and emphases in reaction to these authors, as Schutz expressed them through underlining, marginal arrows, and comments. In addition to the manuscripts, there are memoranda on the graduate faculty of the New School for Social Research; correspondence with R. H. Williame, Felix Kaufmann, Marvin Farber, Robert Heilbroner, Albert Salomon, Talcott Parsons, Eric Voegelin, Aron Gurwitsch, and Harold Garfinkel;

contributions from the Troisième Colloque Philosophique de Royaumont; and short notes on such figures of note as Simmel, Sombart, Weber, and Durkheim.

The following insights into Schutz, of value for this book, were suggested by sections of the archive that follow: Before Schutz wrote *Der sinnhafte Aufbau der sozialen Welt,* he was giving serious consideration to the limits of self-interpretation and the interpretation of the Other and to the context in which reflective and scientific attitudes are embedded. "Vorstudien zu: *Der sinnhafte Aufbau der sozialen Welt,*" 1 : 1–37.

Throughout the archive, Schutz continually asks from which viewpoints claims are being made in line with the crucial distinction between the subjective and objective viewpoints. Schutz finds this central distinction operative in the definition of culture ("T. S. Eliot's Concept of Culture," 57, 7478–7517, 11117–41) and in the joke ("Über den Witz," 46, EI no. 69, 7036–53). Schutz gives attention to the perspective from which claims are made, cf. "Studien zu Talcott Parsons: The Structure of Social Action," 4, no. 25, 178–94; "The Theory of Social Role," B1, EI no. 1 (spring term, 1956), 7609–7774; "The Theory of Social Group," B2, EI no. 2 (spring term, 1954), 7775–8050; "Social Action," B3, EI no. 3/4 (1943/44 respective of 1954), 8051–8205; "Equality, Prejudice, and Discrimination," B10, EI no. 11 (fall term, 1956), 9825–9935; "The Stranger," B12, EI no. 16, 10135–10286.

The mere volume of work dedicated to Scheler in the archive indicates that he was more important to Schutz than a glance at Schutz's published work might suggest (four folders, 557 pages). In addition to giving insights into Scheler's motivation [cf. "Other Minds," B4, EI no. 6/7 (spring term, 1957), 8206–8648, especially, 8579, and "Contemporary European Philosophy," B16, EI no. 15, 10611–10802, especially, 10723], Schutz's archival comments and citations of influences and Scheler and Scheler's critics make it possible to see how Scheler's a priori *ordre du coeur* replaced Kant's rationalized approach to feeling and how Schutz transposed this hierarchized order into his socially determined, relative relevance systems. Cf. "On Max Scheler's Epistemology and Ethics," 8, EI no. 30, 1285–1414; "Scheler's Theory of Intersubjectivity," 9, EI no. 31, 1415–1614; "Max Scheler," 10, EI no. 32, 1615–87; "Max Scheler," 11, EI no. 33, 1688–1842.

There are numerous suggestions of the architectonic organization of the social sciences that Schutz envisioned, with *Der sinnhafte Aufbau der sozialen Welt* as foundational for higher level, autonomous social sciences. Cf. "Untersuchungen über Grundbegriffe und Methoden der Sozialwissenschaften," 50, 7212–30; "Zur Nationalökonomie," 11, EI no. 33, 1688–1842.

The subtle alteration of experience introduced by reflection on it emerges from Schutz's consideration of William James. Cf. "Bergson/James," B17, EI no. 19, 10803–11044.

The lecture and seminar files clearly reveal how Schutz critically applied his findings in *Der sinnhafte Aufbau der sozialen Welt* to assorted sociological and philosophical topics (for example, social role, social group theory, the problem of self and society, the stranger, other minds, symbolism, and language). They also show how Schutz's own philosophical base enabled him to criticize major personages in American sociology and Anglo-American philosophy. Of special interest are Schutz's encounter with G. H. Mead [cf. "Self and Society," B9, EI no. 11 (fall term, 1957), 9547–9824], his analysis of the sociohistorical determination of such symbols as the crucifix (cf. "Sign and Symbol I," B7, EI no. 9, 9173–9326; "Sign and Symbol II," B8, EI no. 10, 9327–9546), as well as the broader social context of language that fulfills many more functions than simple reference [cf. "Sociology of Language" (Notes by Helmut Wagner), B14, 10527–55].

Schutz was adept at finding echoes of his theory of action in literature just as he was able to discover a literary correlate to his theory of multiple realities in "Don Quixote and the Problem of Reality" in his published works, *Collected Papers*, vol. 2. Cf. "Wilhelm Meisters Lehrjahre," 52, EI no. 21, 7275–7334.

Schutz's stress on the *ego agens*, the role of affect in cognition, and horizonal character of consciousness is evident in his "Das Problem der Personalität in der Sozialwelt," 48, EI no. 20, and 49, 7060–7211 [includes "erstes Manuskript" (Weitlaubrunn, Juli/Aug., 1936), 48, EI no. 20, 7060–7101; "Die Einheit des Leibes" (31.7.1937), 49, 7102–33; "Die Tempora des Ich" (13.8.1937), 7134–58; "Die Konstitution der Wirkwelt und ihrer Modifikationen" (Kanzelhöhe, 25.8.1937), 7159–88; "Die Welt des Traumes" (Kanzelhöhe, 26–27.8.1937), 7189–7211]. Many of these same ideas, however, find expression in Schutz's later published essay "On Multiple Realities," *Collected Papers*, 1:207–59.

Finally, the archive makes accessible Schutz's own extensive and concise comments on the values and limitations of Husserl's thought, although most of these can also be located in the published sources. Cf. "Husserl, Ideen II und III," 25, EI no. 48, 5222–5498; "Rezensionen," 55, EI no. 73, 7398–7426, particularly, "AS: Husserl, *Formale und transzendentale Logik*," (April, 1933), 7398–7403; "AS: Husserl, *Méditations Cartésiennes*," (Dec. 1932), 7404–10.

Works about Schutz

Barber, Michael. "Alfred Schut'z Methodology and the Paradox of the Sociology of Knowledge." *Philosophy Today* 30 (1986):58–65.

———. "Constitution and the Sedimentation of the Social in Alfred Schutz's Theory of Typification." *The Modern Schoolman* 54 (1987):111–20.

Cox, Ronald. *Schutz's Theory of Relevance: A Phenomenological Critique*. Hague: Martinus Nijhoff, 1978.

Gorman, Robert. *The Dual Vision: Alfred Schutz and the Myth of Phenomenological Science*. Boston: Routledge and Kegan Paul, 1977.

Grathoff, Richard, and Walter M. Sprondel, eds. *Alfred Schütz und die Idee des Alltags in den Sozialwissenschaften*. Stuttgart: F. Enke Verlag, 1979.

Grathaff, Richard, and Bernhard Waldenfels, eds. *Sozialität und Intersubjektivität: Phänomenologische Perspektiven der Sozialwissenschaften im Umkreis von Aron Gurwitsch und Afred Schütz*. Munich: Wilhelm Fink, 1983.

Gurwitsch, Aron. "The Common-Sense World As Social Reality: A Discussion of Alfred Schutz." *Social Research* 29 (1962): 50–72.

Horowitz, Ruth L. "Phenomenology and Citizenship: A Contribution by Alfred Schutz." *Philosophy and Phenomenological Research* 38 (1977):293–311.

Kersten, Fred. "Alfred Schutz on Social Theory." *Annals of Phenomenological Sociology* 1 (1976):57–66.

Natanson, Maurice. "Alfred Schutz." In *International Encyclopedia of the Social Sciences*, edited by David L. Sills, Vol. 14. New York: Macmillan, 1968.

———. "Alfred Schutz on Social Reality and Social Science." *Social Research* 35 (1968):217–44.

———. *Anonymity: A Study in the Philosophy of Alfred Schutz*. Bloomington: Indiana University Press, 1986.

———. "Phenomenology and Typification: A Study in the Philosophy of Alfred Schutz." *Social Research* 37 (1970):1–22.

————. "The Phenomenology of Alfred Schutz." *Inquiry* 9(1966):157–65.

Natanson, Maurice, ed. *Phenomenology and Social Reality: Essays in Memory of Alfred Schutz.* Hague: Martinus Nijhoff, 1970.

Stonier, Alfred, and Karl Bode "A New Approach to the Methodology of the Social Sciences." *Economica* 4 (1937): 406–24.

Thomason, Burke C. *Making Sense of Reification: Alfred Schutz and Constructionist Theory.* London: Macmillan, 1982.

Voegelin, Eric. "In Memoriam Alfred Schütz" and "Brief an Alfred Schütz über Edmund Husserl." In *Anamnesis: Zur Theorie der Geschichte und Politik.* Munich: Piper, 1966.

Wagner, Helmut. *Alfred Schutz: An Intellectual Biography.* Chicago: University of Chicago Press, 1983.

————. "The Bergsonian Period of Alfred Schutz." *Philosophy and Phenomenological Research* 38 (1977):187–99.

————. "Phenomenology and Contemporary Sociological Theory: The Contribution of Alfred Schutz." *Sociological Focus* 2 (1969):73–86.

Wagner, Helmut, with Ilja Srubar. *A Bergsonian Bridge to Phenomenological Psychology.* Washington, D.C.: Center for Advanced Research in Phenomenology and University Press of America, 1984.

Webb, Rodman B. *The Presence of the Past: John Dewey and Alfred Schutz on the Genesis and Organization of Experience.* Gainesville: University Presses of Florida, 1976.

Williame, Robert. *Les Fondements Phénoménologigues de la Sociologie Compréhensive: Alfred Schutz et Max Weber.* Hague: Martinus Nijoff, 1973.

Wolff, Kurt H., ed. *Alfred Schutz: Appraisals and Developments.* Dordrecht: Martinus Nijhoff, 1984.

Zaner, Richard. "Theory of Intersubjectivity: Alfred Schutz.: *Social Research* 28 (1961):71–94.

Related Works

Adorno, T. W., E. Frenkel-Brunswick, D. J. Levinson, and R. N Sanford. *The Authoritarian Personality.* New York: Norton, 1950

Barnes, Barry. "On the Conventional Character of Knowledge and Cognition." *Philosophy of the Social Sciences* 11(1981):303–33.

Berger, Peter, and Thomas Luckmann. *The Social Construction of Reality: A Treatise in the Sociology of Knowledge.* Garden City, N.Y.: Doubleday, 1966.

Bergson, Henri. *Essai sur les Données Immédiates de la Conscience.* Paris: F. Alcan, 1889. Authorized translation by F. L. Pogson, under the title *Time and Free Will: An Essay on the Immediate Data of Consciousness.* London: George Allen & Unwin and New York: The Macmillan Company, 1950.

Bernstein, Richard. *The Restructuring of Social and Political Theory.* Philadelphia: University of Pennsylvania Press, 1978.

Bloor, David. *Knowledge and Social Imagery.* London and Boston: Routledge and Kegan Paul, 1976.

Brodbeck, May, ed. *Readings in the Philosophy of the Social Sciences.* New York: Macmillan, 1968.

Connerton, Paul, ed. *Critical Sociology: Selected Readings.* New York: Penguin, 1976.

Cooley, Charles Horton. *Human Nature and the Social Order.* Rev. ed. New York: Scribners, 1922.

Cunningham, Suzanne. *Language and the Phenomenological Reductions of Edmund Husserl.* Hague: Martinus Nijhoff, 1976.

Curtis, James E., and John W. Petras, eds. *The Sociology of Knowledge: A Reader.* New York: Præger, 1970.

Dallmayr, Fred R., and Thomas A. McCarthy, eds. *Understanding and Social Inquiry.* Notre Dame, Ind.: University of Notre Dame Press, 1977.

Danziger, K. "Ideology and Utopia in South Africa: A Methodological Contribution to the Sociology of Knowledge." In *Towards the Sociology of Knowledge: Origin and Development of a Sociological Thought Style,* edited by Gunter W. Remmling, London: Routledge and Kegan Paul, 1973.

DeGré, Gerard. *Society and Ideology: An Inquiry into the Sociology of Knowledge.* New York: Columbia University Bookstore, 1943.

Derrida, Jacques. *Speech and Phenomena, and Other Essays on Husserl's Theory of Signs.* Translated by David B. Allison. Evanston, Ill.: Northwestern University Press, 1973.

Dilthey, Wilhelm. *Descriptive Psychology and Historical Understanding.* Translated by Richard M. Zaner and Kenneth L. Heiges. Hague: Martinus Nijhoff, 1977.

———. *Die geistige Welt.* Edited by Georg Misch. Vol. 5 of *Gesammelte Schriften.* Leipzig: B. G. Teubner and Göttingen: Vandenhoeck and Ruprecht, 1924.

Durkheim, Emile. *The Rules of Sociological Method.* 8th ed. Translated by Sarah A. Solovay and John H. Mueller and edited by George E. G. Catlin. Glencoe, Ill.: Free Press, 1958.

———. *Suicide: A Study in Sociology.* Translated by John A. Spaulding and George Simpson and edited by George Simpson. Glencoe, Ill.: Free Press, 1951.

Elveton, R. O., ed. *The Phenomenology of Husserl: Selected Critical Readings.* Translated by R. O. Elveton. Chicago: Quadrangle Books, 1970.

Embree, Lester, ed. *Essays in Memory of Aron Gurwitsch.* Washington, D.C.: Center for Advanced Research in Phenomenology and University Press of American, 1984.

Engels, Friedrich. *Briefe.* Vols. 37, 39 of *Werke* by Karl Marx and Friedrich Engels. Berlin: Dietz, 1956–68.

———. "Letters" in *Selected Works* or Karl Marx and Friedrich Engels, New York: International Publishers, 1968.

———. *Ludwig Feuerbach and the End of Classical German Philosophy.* In *Selected Works* of Karl Marx and Friedrich Engels, New York: International Publishers, 1968.

———. *Ludwig Feuerbach und der Ausgang der klassischen deutschen Philosophie.* Vol. 21 of *Werke* by Karl Marx and Friedrich Engels, Berlin: Dietz, 1956–68.

Fahrenbach, Helmut, ed. *Wirklichkeit und Reflexion: Walter Schulz zum 60. Geburtstag.* Pfullingen: Neske, 1973.

Fink, Eugen. "Operative Concepts in Husserl's Phenomenology." In *A Priori and World: European Contributions to Husserlian Phenomenology.* Edited and translated by William McKenna, Robert M. Harlan, and Laurence E. Winters. Hague: Martinus Nijoff, 1981.

————. "The Phenomenological Philosophy of Edmund Husserl and Contemporary Criticism." In *The Phenomenology of Edmund Husserl, Selected Critical Readings*, edited and translated by R. O. Elveton, Chicago: Quadrangle Books, 1970.

Foucault, Michel. *The Archeology of Knowledge.* Translated by A. M. Sheridan Smith. New York: Harper and Row, 1972.

————. *The Order of Things: An Archeology of the Human Sciences.* New York: Pantheon, 1970.

Geertz, Clifford. *The Interpretation of Cultures: Selected Essays.* New York: Basic Books, 1973.

Gilligan, Carol. "Woman's Place in Man's Life Cycle." *Harvard Educational Review* 49 (1979):431–45.

Grünwald, Ernst. *Das Problem der Soziologie des Wissens: Versuch einer kritischen Darstellung der wissenssoziologischen Theorien.* Wien-Leipzig: Wilhelm Braumüller, 1934.

Gurwitsch, Aron. *The Field of Consciousness.* Pittsburgh: Duquesne University Press, 1964.

Habermas, Jürgen. *Communication and the Evolution of Society.* Translated by Thomas McCarthy. London: Heinemann, 1976.

————. *Knowledge and Human Interests.* 2d ed. Translated by Jeremy J. Shapiro. London: Heinemann, 1972.

————. "Wahrheitstheorien." In *Wirklichkeit und Reflexion: Walter Schulz zum 60. Geburtstag*, edited by Helmut Fahrenbach. Pfullingen: Neske, 1973.

————. *Zur Logik der Sozialwissenschaften.* Tübingen: J. C. B. Mohr (Paul Siebeck), 1967.

Hansberry, Lorraine. *A Raisin in the Sun.* New York: Random House, 1959.

Hartung, Frank E. "Problems of the Sociology of Knowledge." In *The Sociology of Knowledge: A Reader*, edited by James E. Curtis and John W. Petras. New York: Praeger, 1970.

Hayes-Bautista, David E. "Chicano Patients and Medical Practitioners: A Sociology of Knowledge Paradigm of Lay-Professional Interaction." *Social Science and Medicine* 12 (1978):83–90.

Hegel, G. W. F. *Philosophy of Right.* Translated by T. M. Knox. Oxford: Oxford University Press, 1967.

Homans, George C. "Bringing Men Back In." In *The Philosophy of Social Explanation*, edited by Alan Ryan. London: Oxford University Press, 1973.

Horowitz, Irving Louis. *Philosophy, Science, and the Sociology of Knowledge.* Springfield, Ill.: Charles C. Thomas, 1961.

Hoyos Vásquez, Guillermo. *Intentionalität als Verantwortung: Geschichtsteleologie und Teleologie der Intentionalität bei Husserl.* Hague: Martinus Nijhoff, 1976.

Husserl, Edmund. *Cartesian Meditations: An Introduction to Phenomenology.* Translated by Dorion Cairns. Hague: Martinus Nijhoff, 1960.

————. *The Crisis of European Sciences and Transcendental Phenomenology: An Introduction to Phenomenological Philosophy.* Edited by Walter Biemel and translated by David Carr. Evanston, Ill.: Northwestern University Press, 1970.

————. *Erfahrung und Urteil: Untersuchungen zur Genealogie der Logik.* Hamburg: Classen, 1964. Translated by James S. Churchill and Karl Ameriks under the title *Experience and Judgment: Investigations in a Genealogy of Logic.* Evanston, Ill.: Northwestern University Press, 1973.

―――. *Gessammelte Werke.* Vol. 3, *Ideen zu einer reinen Phänomenologie und phänomenologische Philosophie.* Book 1: *Allgemeine Einfuhrung in die reine Phänomenologie.* Edited by Karl Schuhmann. Hague: Martinus Nijhoff, 1976. Vol. 4, *Ideen zu einer reinen Phänomenologie und phänomenologische Philosophie.* Book 2: *Phänomenologische Untersuchungen zur Konstitution.* Edited by Marly Biemel. Hague: Martinus Nijhoff, 1952. Vol. 7, *Erste Philosophie (1923/24),* part 1, *Kritische Ideengeschichte.* Edited by Rudolf Boehm. Hague: Martinus Nijhoff, 1956. Vol. 8, *Erste Philosophie (1923/24),* part 2, *Theorie der phänomenologischen Reduktion,* edited by Rudolf Boehm. Hague: Martinus Nijhoff, 1959. Vol. 10, *Zur Phänomenologie des Inneren Zeitbewusstseins (1893–1917).* Edited by Rudolf Boehm. Hague: Martinus Nijhoff, 1966. Vol. 11, *Analysen zur passiven Synthesis, aus Vorlesungs- und Forschungsmanuskripten, 1918–1926,* edited by Margot Fleischer. Hague: Martinus Nijhoff, 1966.

―――. *Ideas Pertaining to a Pure Phenomenology and to a Phenomenological Philosophy.* Book 1, *General Introduction to a Pure Phenomenology.* Translated by F. Kersten. Hague: Martinus Nijhoff, 1982.

―――. *Logical Investigations.* Translated from the 2d Ger. ed. by J. N. Findlay. New York: Humanities Press, 1970.

―――. "Nachwort zu meinen 'Ideen zu einer reinen Phänomenologie und phänomenologischen Philosophie.'" *Jahrbuch für Philosophie und phänomenologische Forschung* 11 (1930):549–70.

―――. *Phenomenological Psychology.* Translated by John Scanlon. Hague: Martinus Nijhoff, 1977.

―――. *The Phenomenology of Internal Time-Consciousness.* Edited by Martin Heidegger and translated by James S. Churchill. Bloomington: Indiana University Press, 1964.

―――. *Philosophy As Rigorous Science.* In *Phenomenology and the Crisis of Philosophy,* translated by Quentin Lauer, New York: Harper and Row, 1965.

Husserl, Edmund, and Wilhelm Dilthey. "Correspondencia entre Dilthey y Husserl." *Revista de Filosofía de la Universidad de Costa Rica* 1 (1957):101–24.

Jones, Robert Alun, ed. 1978–83. *Research in Sociology of Knowledge, Sciences and Art: An Annual Compilation of Research.* 4 vols. Greenwich, Conn.: Jai Press.

Jules-Rosette, Bënetta. "The Veil of Objectivity: Prophecy, Divination, and Social Inquiry." *American Anthropologist* 80 (1978):549–70.

Kennedy, Emmet. *A Philosophe in the Age of Revolution: Destutt de Tracy and the Origins of "Ideology."* Philadelphia: American Philosophical Society, 1978.

Kersten, Fred. "Phenomenology, History, Myth." In *Phenomenology and Social Reality: Essays in Memory of Alfred Schutz,* edited by Maurice Natanson. Hague: Martinus Nijhoff, 1970.

Krimerman, Leonard I., ed. *The Nature and Scope of Social Science.* New York: Appleton-Century-Crofts, 1969.

Kripke, Saul. "Identity and Necessity." In *Naming, Necessity, and Natural Kinds,* edited by Stephen P. Schwartz. Ithaca, N.Y.: Cornell University Press, 1977.

Levinas, Emmanuel. *Totality and Infinity: An Essay on Exteriority.* Translated by Alphonso Lingis. Hague: Martinus Nijhoff, 1969.

Machlup, Fritz. *Knowledge: Its Creation, Distribution, and Economic Significance.* Vol.

1, *Knowledge and Knowledge Production*. Princeton: Princeton: Princeton University Press, 1980.

———. *The Production and Distribution of Knowledge in the United States*. Princeton: Princeton University Press, 1962.

Machlup, Fritz, and Kenneth Leeson. *Information through the Printed Word: The Dissemination of Scholarly, Scientific, and Intellectual Knowledge*. 4 vols. New York: Praeger, 1978–80.

Makkreel, Rudolf A. *Dilthey: Philosopher of the Human Studies*. Princeton: Princeton University Press. 1975.

Mannheim, Karl. *Essays on the Sociology of Knowledge*. Translated and edited by Paul Kecskemeti New York: Oxford University Press, 1952.

———. *Ideology and Utopia: An Introduction to the Sociology of Knowledge*. Translated by Louis Wirth and Edward Shils. London: Kegan Paul, Trench, Trubner, and Co., 1936.

———. *Structures of Thinking*. Edited by David Kettler, Volker Meja, and Nico Stehr, and translated by Jeremy Shapiro and Shierry Weber Nicholsen. London: Routledge and Kegan Paul, 1982.

Marx, Karl. "Contribution to the Critique of Hegel's Philosophy of Right." In *Early Writings*, translated and edited by T. B. Bottomore. New York: McGraw-Hill, 1964.

———. *Early Writings*. Translated and edited by T. B. Bottomore. New York: McGraw-Hill, 1964.

———. "Preface to *A Contribution to the Critique of Political* Economy." In *Selected Works* by Karl Marx and Friedrich Engels. New York: International Publishers.

———. *Writings of the Young Marx on Philosophy and Society*. Edited and translated by Loyd D. Easton and Kurt H. Guddat. Garden City, N.Y.: Anchor, 1967.

Marx, Karl, and Friedrich Engels. *The German Ideology: A Critique of the Most Recent German Philosophy As Represented by Feuerbach, B. Bauer, and Stirner*. In *Writings of the Young Marx on Philosophy and Society*, edited and translated by Loyd D. Easton and Kurt H. Guddat. Garden City, N.Y.: Anchor, 1967.

———. *Selected Works*. New York: International Publishers, 1968.

———. *Werke*. Berlin: Dietz, 1956–68. Vol. 1, "Zur Kritik der Hegelschen Rechtsphilosophie." Vol. 3, *Die deutsche Ideologie: Kritik der neuesten deutschen Philosophie in ihrer Repräsentanten, Feuerbach, B. Bauer, und Stirner und des deutschen Sozialismus in seinen verschiedenen Propheten*. Vol. 13, *Zur Kritik der politischen Ökonomie*. Vol. 21, *Ludwig Feuerbach und der Ausgang der klassischen deutschen Philosophie. Briefe*, vols. 37, 39.

McCarthy, Thomas. *The Critical Theory of Jürgen Habermas*. Cambridge: MIT Press, 1978.

McKenna, William, Robert M. Harlan, and Laurence Winters, eds. and trans. *A Priori and World: European Contributions to Husserlian Phenomenology*. Hague and Boston: Martinus Nijhoff, 1981.

Mead, George Herbert. *Mind, Self and Society, from the Standpoint of a Social Behaviorist*. Edited by Charles W. Morris. Chicago: University of Chicago Press, 1934.

Merleau-Ponty, Maurice. *Phenomenology of Perception*. Translated by Colin Smith. New York: Humanities Press, 1962.

———. "The Philosopher and Sociology." In *Signs*, translated by Richard C. McCleary. Evanston, Ill.: Northwestern University Press, 1964.

———. *Signs*. Translated by Richard C. McCleary. Evanston, Ill.: Northwestern University Press, 1964.

Merton, Robert K. "Paradigm for the Sociology of Knowledge." In *The Sociology of Knowledge: A Reader,* edited by James E. Curtis and John W. Petras. New York and Washington: Praeger, 1970.

———. *Social Theory and Social Structure.* Rev. and enl. ed. Glenceo, Ill.: Free Press, 1957.

———. *The Sociology of Science: Theoretical and Empirical Investigations.* Edited by Norman W. Storer. Chicago and London: University of Chicago Press, 1973.

Mills, C. Wright. *Power, Politics and People: The Collected Essays of C. Wright Mills.* Edited by Irving Louis Horowitz. New York: Oxford University Press, 1963.

Nagel, Ernest. "Symposium: Problems of Concept and Theory Formation in the Social Sciences." In *Science, Language, and Human Rights.* Vol. 1, [*Proceedings of*] *American Philosophical Association, Eastern Division.* Philadelphia: University of Pennsylvania Press, 1952.

Natanson, Maurice. "Descriptive Phenomenology." In *Essays in Memory of Aron Gurwitsch*, edited by Lester Embree. Washington, D.C.: Center for Advanced Research in Phenomenology and University Press of America, 1984.

———. *Edmund Husserl: Philosopher of Infinite Tasks.* Evanston, Ill.: Northwestern University Press, 1973.

———. *The Journeying Self: A Study in Philosophy and Social Role.* Reading, Mass.: Addison-Wesley, 1970.

———. *Literature, Philosophy, and the Social Sciences: Essays in Existentialism and Phenomenology.* Hague: Martinus Nijhoff, 1962.

———. "Phenomenology, Typificiation, and the World As Taken for Granted." In *Philomathēs: Studies and Essays in the Humanities in Memory of Philip Merlan,* edited by Robert R. Palmer and Robert Hamerton-Kelly. Hague: Martinus Nijhoff, 1970.

Ortega y Gasset, José. *Man and People.* Authorized translation by R. Trask. New York: Norton, 1957.

Palmer, Robert B., and Robert Hamerton-Kelly, eds. *Philomathēs: Studies and Essays in the Humanities in Memory of Philip Merlan.* Hague: Martinus Nijhoff, 1970.

Parsons, Talcott. "An Approach to the Sociology of Knowledge." In *The Sociology of Knowledge: A Reader,* edited by James E. Curtis and John W. Petras. New York and Washington, D.C.: Praeger, 1970.

———. *The Structure of Social Action: A Study in Social Theory with Special Reference to a Group of Recent European Writers.* New York: Free Press, 1968.

Rang, Bernhard. *Kausalität und Motivation: Untersuchungen vom Verhältnis von Perspektivität und Objektivität in der Phänomenologie Edmund Husserls.* Hague: Martinus Nijhoff, 1973.

Remmling, Gunter W., ed. *Towards the Sociology of Knowledge: Origins and Development of a Sociological Thought Style.* New York: Appleton-Century-Crofts, 1967.

Ricoeur, Paul. *Husserl: An Analysis of His Phenomenology.* Translated by Edward G. Ballard and Lester E. Embree. Evanston, Ill.: Northwestern University Press, 1967.

Rickert, Heinrich. *Science and History: A Critique of Positivist Epistemology.* Translated by George Reisman and edited by Arthur Goddard. Princeton, N.J.: Van Nostrand, 1962.

Runciman, W. G. *A Treatise on Social Theory.* Vol. 1, *The Methodology of Social Theory.* Cambridge and New York: Cambridge University Press, 1983.

Ryan, Alan, ed. *The Philosophy of Social Explanation.* London and New York: Oxford University Press, 1973.

Scheler, Max. *Formalism in Ethics and Non-formal Ethics of Values: A New Attempt toward the Formulation of an Ethical Personalism.* Translated by Manfred S. Frings and Roger L. Funk. Evanston, Ill.: Northwestern University Press, 1977.

———. *Man's Place in Nature.* Translated by Hans Meyerhoff. Boston: Beacon, 1961.

———. *The Nature of Sympathy.* Translated by Peter Heath. Hamden, Conn.: Archon Books, 1970.

———. *Problems of a Sociology of Knowledge.* Translated by Manfred S. Frings and edited by Kenneth W. Stikkers. London: Routledge & Kegan Paul, 1980.

———. *Schriften zur Soziologie und Weltanschauungslehre.* vol. 1, *Moralia.* Vol. 2, *Nation und Weltanschauung.* Vol. 3, *Christentum und Gesellschaft.* Leipzig: P. Reinhold, 1923.

———. *Die Wissensformen und die Gesellschaft.* Leipzig: Der Neue Geist, 1926.

Schelting, Alexander Von. *Max Webers Wissenschaftslehre: Das logische Problem der historischen Kulturerkenntnis; die Grenzen der Soziologie des Wissens.* Tübingen: J. C. B. Mohr (Paul Siebeck), 1934.

Schwartz, Stephen P., ed. *Naming, Necessity, and Natural Kinds.* Ithaca, N.Y.: Cornell University Press, 1977.

Sills, David L., ed. *International Encyclopedia of the Social* Sciences. 17 vols. New York: Macmillan, 1968.

Simmel, Georg. *Conflict.* Translated by Kurt H. Wolff. New York: Free Press, 1955.

———. *The Web of Group Affiliations.* Translated by Reinhard Bendix. New York: Free Press, 1955.

Stark, Werner. *The Sociology of Knowledge: An Essay in Aid of a Deeper Understanding of the History of Ideas.* Glencoe, Ill.: Free Press, 1958.

Theunissen, Michael. *The Other: Studies in the Social Ontology of Husserl, Heidegger, Sartre, and Buber.* Translated by Christopher Macann. Cambridge and London: MIT Press, 1984.

Wash, Joachim. *Das Verstehen: Grundzüge einer Geschichte der hermeneutischen Theorie im 19. Jahrhundert.* Vol. 1, *Die grossen Systeme.* Vol. 2, *Die theologische Hermeneutik von Schleiermacher bis Hoffman.* Tübingen: J. C. B. Mohr (Paul Siebeck), 1926–33.

Weber, Max *Economy and Society: An Outline of Interpretive Sociology.* Translated by Ephraim Fischoff and others and edited by Guenther Roth and Claus Wittich. 2 vols. Berkeley: University of California Press, 1978.

———. *From Max Weber: Essays in Sociology.* Translated and edited by H. H. Gerth and C. Wright Mills. New York: Oxford University Press, 1946.

———. *The Methodology of the Social Sciences.* Translated and edited by Edward A. Shils and Henry A. Finch. New York: Free Press, 1949.

———. *The Protestant Ethic and the Spirit of Capitalism.* Translated by Talcott Parsons. New York: Scribners, 1958.

Weinstein, Deena, and Michael Weinstein. "Sociologies of Knowledge As Rhetorical Strategies." *Free Inquiry* 6 (1978): 1–14.

———. "The Sociology of Nonknowledge: A Paradigm." In *Research in Sociology of Knowledge, Sciences and Art: An Annual Compilation of Research,* edited by Robert Alun Jones. Greenwich, Conn.: Jai Press, 1978.

Windelband, Wilhelm. *Geschichte und Naturwissenschaften: Rede gehalten von dem Rektor.* Strassburg: Das Stiftungfest der Kaiser-Wilhelms-Universität, 1894.

Znaniecki, Florian. *The Social Role of the Man of Knowledge.* New York: Columbia University Press, 1940.

Index

Abstraction: and the sociology of knowledge, 97

Act, 106 n.10

Action: based on project, 30, 35, 53; categories for describing, 97; defined, 106 n.10; taken for granted by social sciences, 62–63; Weber's theory of, 26, 30

Adorno, T. W., 110 n.29

Affect, 12, 36, 106 n.17

Affectual behavior, 28

Analogy theory of other minds, 20, 23

Analysts, 59

Anomalies. *See* Predictability

Anonymity: of origins of socially derived knowledge, 59; in our experience of contemporaries, 54; produced by categories of meaning, 44, 46; of scientific types, 73–74, 97; of social world to a detached observer, 29; within different orientations within the social world, 104 n.35

Appresentation, 23, 25

Architectonic, 11–12, 95–98, 104 n.24, 117–18 n.33, 118 n.34

Bacon, Francis, 9, 92

Barnes, Barry, 12, 114 n.21, 115 n.6

Because motive: and eidetic claims, 11, 85–87; hermeneutically determined, 87; indicative of Schutz's sympathy with sociological relativism, 90–92; neglected by Weber, 32; and relevance, 38; and truth claims, 90; useful for sociology of knowledge, 97; and validity criteria, 90

Behavior. *See* Conduct

Berger, Peter, 12, 118 n.34; and Thomas Luckmann, *The Social Construction of Reality,* 118 n.34

Bergson, Henri, 40, 98

Bergsonian period of Alfred Schutz, 40, 107 n.27

Biemel, Marly, 75

Biographical situation: historical uniqueness of, 40–41; intersubjectively determined, 45–46, 57–61; relevances and typifications in, 37, 51–53; removal from, by social scientist, 67, 70–71

Bloor, David, 12

Body, the, 10, 22–24, 46, 73

Brown, Justice Henry B., 58

Causal explanation, 26, 50, 104 n.24, 109 n.4

Cave, Plato's, 9, 92

Collected Papers 2, 32

Commentators, 59

Communication, 43–44, 62–63, 104 n.35

"Concept and Theory Formation in the Social Sciences," 66–67

Conduct, 30, 35

Conscience collective, 99, 119 n.41

Consciousness of, 22, 24–25, 64

Consociates, 61

Constitution, 75–77

Constructs of common sense thinking: constructs of, 67, 69, 95

Contemporaries, 29, 47, 51, 56, 61, 73

Cooley, Charles Horton, 43

Course of action patterns, 50, 68

Cox, Ronald, 106 n.10

Crisis of European Sciences and Transcendental Phenomenology, The (Husserl), 63, 106 n.12

Derrida, Jacques, 65

Dewey, John, 102 n.8

Dilthey, Wilhelm: correspondence between Husserl and, 76; empathy theory of, 19; and nexus of experi-

132